A GLASS HALF FULL

Felix Dennis

A GLASS HALF FULL

Illustrations by Bill Sanderson

HUTCHINSON
LONDON

First published in 2002 by
Hutchinson

The Random House Group Ltd
20 Vauxhall Bridge Road, SW1V 2SA

Random House Australia (Pty) Ltd
20 Alfred Street, Milsons Point, Sydney
New South Wales, Australia

Random House New Zealand Ltd
18 Poland Street, Glenfield,
Auckland, New Zealand

Random House South Africa (Pty) Ltd
Endulini, 5A Jubilee Road, Parktown 2193, South Africa

A CIP catalogue record for this book is available from the British Library

ISBN 0091795338

Papers used by Random House are natural, recyclable
products made from wood grown in sustainable forests.
The manufacturing processes conform to the environmental
regulations of the country of origin.

Set in Adobe Electra
Printed and bound in Great Britain by
Butler & Tanner Ltd, Frome and London

Cover Design by Richard Adams
Book Design by Mike Dunn

To my indomitable mother,
Dorothy Grace Sawyer

And to the companion of my heart,
Marie-France Demolis

"If it's a good idea, go ahead and do it.
It's much easier to apologise than it is to get permission."
— *Rear Admiral Grace Murray Hopper (1906-1992)*

But as I raved and grew more fierce and wild
At every word,
Methought I heard one calling, *Child!*
And I replied, *My Lord.*
— *George Herbert (1593 - 1633)*

Contents

3	Travel Advisory
4	Never Go Back
5	The Unexpected Guest
6	Advice to a Godson Leaving Home
6	Snakes and Ladders
7	White Vase
8	The True Interpretation of American Signs and Announcements
9	A Silent Prayer...
10	The Baby Boomers
11	Ship's Cat
12	What Lies Hidden
14	The Gardeners
15	The Mergansers
16	The Patrician
17	On Domestication of Any Kind
18	A Digital Prayer
19	Place a Mirror by a Tree
20	Our Lady in White
21	The Greatest Gift
22	The Man Who Built Mustique
24	Autumn Harvest
25	Skate Mates
26	Craft
26	The Worm at the End of the World
28	No-Man's Land
29	To A God Child
31	Udde~Well Pond
32	Eureka
32	An IBM Engineer Makes A Service Call
35	The Don
36	Snakeskin Boots
37	As the wheel turns...
38	Dress Rehearsals
39	It was always Sunday morning...
40	My Grandfather's Bicycle
41	A Child of Adam and Eve
42	Last Supper
43	Freeze!
44	Assailed by life...
44	Boy Meets Girl
44	Dreams
45	The Mask
45	Guests
46	The Ministry Cull
48	On News of a Friend's Sudden Death
49	Nebuchadnezzar
50	Green-eyed Monsters
51	The Biter Bit
53	The Devil to Pay
53	Roll Up! Roll Up!
54	A Glass Half Empty
55	Sylva Anathema
56	If half the world were deaf...
56	The Better Man
58	A Hymn of Hate
60	Telling Lies
61	Passing a School Playground
63	As I spied swallows scything...
64	Five and a Bit
65	Sonnet for H20
67	Sonnet for Bob Dylan On His 60th Birthday
68	The Name of a Man

69	Executive Decisions	102	Spot the Difference
70	I Never Met A Book	103	When mercy strains your patience
71	In A Soho Garden	103	Knowing isn't doing...
72	Ts'ai Lun at Ch'in Che'eng	104	The Wedding Dress
75	The jacket Elvis loaned me...	105	The Troubles
76	Winning the Lottery	106	Dead White Males
77	Last Words of Punch to Judy	108	The Serpent's Gift
79	The Meeting	109	A Poet's Consolation
80	Misery Guts	109	I had a friend...
81	Queen Elizabeth I Greets a Lord	110	The House that Crack Built...
81	Though Fondness may not fall within our gift...	113	A Discovery in Wandsworth
82	The Weeds of Warwickshire	114	Gulliver Sneesby
84	In the Blood?	115	Why Do They Do it?
85	Specific Gravity	116	A Lullaby for Bottles
86	How To Get Rich	118	Oh, do not call them vultures...
87	Space Craft	118	Scapegoats
88	Life Suport	119	Prodigal Son
89	All the young dudes...	120	The Fool
90	Mother Earth	121	Chinese Whispers
91	Intentions	122	Knowing When To Go
91	Victory!	123	Cause and Effect
92	Waste	124	Marchesa Casati's Party
93	Better Than Sex!	125	Sex With Your Ex
94	Sign To Be Erected At The Gate To Argyle Wood	125	The World'd Last Choir
95	Shields	126	Fast Awake
97	Amazing Grace	127	Mighty the ant to an aphid...
98	Shadow Billy	128	If death knows no dominion...
99	Trouble	129	Surreal Deal
100	An Old Dog Is The Best Dog	130	Aleister
101	The Proof	131	A Norman Priest Dreams of the English
		132	The Shield of Art
		133	What time is it?

135 On Reading Dead Rhymers
136 Here Be Dragons
137 The Protestors
138 The Box
139 To A Beautiful Lady of a Certain Age
140 Soho Sestina
142 Ed
143 Warm Round a Fiver
144 Dead Gods
145 They trouble sleep...
146 Xanadu!
147 Galileo's Dream
149 Breakfast on Mustique
150 The Cremation of Jesus Christ
153 Neither A Lender...
154 I have a secret servant...
155 Sally Alice
156 Two Plants
156 The estuaries of hell...
157 Blues
158 Within a maze...
159 Grand-ma
160 A Confrontation in Dorsington
     Churchyard, January 1924
161 The Door
162 The Bearded Dwarf
164 To cOpy-Editers
165 Whistling Ghosts
165 Winds That Douse the Candle
166 Hail to the gods of America...
167 Bedtime Story
167 Love is not compassion...

168 A World That Was Not There
169 Say this to thyself...
170 Johnson
171 Old Dog, New Trick
172 Fundamentals
173 Charlotte
174 The Lamb Bids the Tyger Farewell
177 Of Walls and Fences
178 Love Came to Visit Me
180 Fin Finis
181 A miser's purse...
182 You may not evil do...
183 She Got What She Wanted
184 Seek-no-further
185 Atlas Shrugs
185 Swim or Float
186 Dream Time
186 God Knows What
187 Though no good deed...
187 Deducing Fairies
188 Neanderthal Nights
189 Seven-legged Spider
190 Telex Memories
191 The Old, Old Error
192 The Snowman
193 In Time of Doubt
194 You!
195 When the boot goes in...
196 Lord North Instructs His Son and Heir...
197 Classic Clichés
199 Flower Power
200 You think it made a difference...

Preface

'Compulsion is an ugly word,
Obsession is its daughter;
Scribble, scribble, scribble —
My muse will give no quarter...'
— The Scribbler

SOMETHING WAS HORRIBLY WRONG. Occasional bouts of tiredness were now daily occurrences. It was becoming increasingly difficult to walk or move my arms. I felt constantly lethargic — alienated from my own bodily functions — as if they were the responsibility and burden of somebody else. My short term memory was shot. My voice was slurring and my face bloated. It was obvious to everyone but myself that I was in trouble.

I had been warned. Gently by Marie-France. More sternly by my old friend Dick Pountain. And, of course, by my mother. Dick was especially insistent that I sounded as if I'd been drinking half the time. Well, perhaps I had been.

My mother, whom I love deeply, but have more than once described to friends as 'a prettier version of Mrs. Thatcher without any of the soft bits' was emphatic: 'You are ill, Felix. Go and see a doctor at once.' Always listen to your mother.

We staggered out of Horseferry Criminal Court, where I had been giving incoherent evidence on behalf of another old mate, intending to join a group of his supporters on their way to drown their sorrows at a riverside pub. But I couldn't walk. Instead, I had my chauffeur bundle me into the car and drive the short distance to the rendezvous where I parked myself on a wall and watched the muddy Thames rolling down to the sea. I wouldn't have fought much had I rolled away with it.

I was thinking of my friend, Mark. The judge had sent him down for three years, despite the combined efforts of numerous, impassioned character witnesses for the defence. Or, perhaps, because of them. Eighteen months (with good behaviour) inside a British prison for a fifty year old professional was no laughing matter. Neither was the fact that I didn't seem able to breathe properly.

Balancing my untasted pint of Bass on the wall, I called out to my personal assistant and asked her to find a doctor. It was four p.m. on a Friday afternoon. Unsurprisingly, Wendy achieved the impossible with infuriating ease. Within an hour I was stripped to my boxer shorts in a Harley Street consulting room with a physician giving me a serious once over. The search had begun.

Clinics, experts, consultants, hospitals, CAT scans, bone scans, ('you have wonderfully sound bones, Mr. Dennis'), X-rays, ultra-sound, blood tests, cardiovascular tests, colonoscopy, coronary angiogram...after the first week I didn't care much any more. Not that I cared much in the beginning — which should have told me something, had I been well enough to think straight.

I had felt this bad only once before in my life, some fourteen years previously, emerging as a celebrity survivor from an outbreak of Legionnaire's disease contracted in Los Angeles. But in that instance it had all been over in 72 hours. Although recovery was slow, I had known I would survive. Some of my fellow victims, all of whom were older than me, never came out of coma. The choice had been simple, as the hospital staff had made brutally clear: '*Go into coma and you die; keep awake and you live*'. I had been up for that.

After a long walk to the edge of an abyss (no bright lights) I had turned and trudged back to the land of the living. To be truthful, I hadn't much liked what I'd seen down there.

But this was worse. Boring, boring, boring. I cannot abide being bored. Sitting on the edge of a bed in yet another clinic, resplendent in a pink nylon gown which I had clumsily fastened the wrong way round, my private parts shaved and my bare feet dangling several inches from the floor, Dorothy Parker's lines from 'Résumé' came into my mind:

> *Razors pain you;*
> *Rivers are damp;*
> *Acids stain you;*
> *And drugs cause cramp;*
> *Guns aren't lawful;*
> *Nooses give;*
> *Gas smells awful;*
> *You might as well live.*

The 'And' at the beginning of line four had always bothered me. Right-ho, I thought. Let's see how I make out with a spot of poetry. Having always read poetry, even as a young man, perhaps this spur-of-the-moment whim was not as surprising as it might have been for most 52-year-old business men. Begging a pen and a pack of sticky Post-it notes from a suspicious nurse, I began to write.

That was September 13, 1999. I know because I automatically inserted the date at the top, as is my habit when jotting notes in the office. I did not write another poem until August 2000, after the first line had paced unbidden within my thoughts for days, like a dog carrying its lead to an absent-minded owner. In October 2000 I began seriously to get down to it, working three to five hours every night, reading, writing or revising poetry. At first, I kept quiet about it, even to close friends. To be honest, I felt like a fool and a fraud.

A year and a half later there are 350 completed poems in my groaning slip file — a file which accompanies me wherever I go. The 'spot of poetry' has become a fully-fledged obsession. It comes each day, relentlessly, in tidal wave after tidal wave. Once, I attempted a week without reading or composing any poetry. I cracked after four days. Marooned in a sea of verse, I do not desire ever to reach land again.

Perhaps I could not even if I wished. The verse is master now. I have found myself scribbling lines in aeroplanes, during business meetings, at dinner parties and even in my sleep. When I am writing verse, it is as though a carapace, formed from long necessity and habit, is slowly dissolving. But if I am gaining something in the process, I am also aware that I am relinquishing a hard-won tunnel vision and the crab-like armour necessary to succeed financially in a naughty world.

It is an unnerving thought, but perhaps, after fifty years or so, I am finally growing up.

Dorsington
May, 2002

(NB: My old mate Mark is out of prison now. I was eventually diagnosed as hypothyroid and have made a full recovery. Here's what happened in between. Oh, and Dorothy Parker was absolutely right about the 'And' — a fact which rapidly emerged while composing my pastiche, 'Travel Advisory'.)

Author's Note

ORIGINALLY, I had intended to present these poems in chronological order of composition — to form a kind of diary. But wiser heads than mine prevailed, so they are jumbled in random order and left undated.

It is strange, though, how a poem becomes inextricably linked in its author's mind with the location of its composition. Thus the reader will find, in tiny type, attributions like Soho (Kingly Street in London); Dorsington (a village in Warwickshire); Candlewood (a lake in Connecticut); New York (49th Street and 2nd Avenue); Mustique (an island in the West Indies) and even '40,000 ft above the Atlantic'.

Publishing a collection of poetry for a cut-and-thrust entrepreneur is a risky business, as anyone skilled in the art of negotiation would tell you. Knowing your enemy's weaknesses and what makes him or her tick is half the battle. For that very reason, I am at least assured of the sale of a hundred or so copies of this little book.

To those destined to sit across a table to negotiate with me in the future, therefore: here is a rival's head on a plate. Make what you will of it! But be sure to check out 'I have a secret servant...' on page 154. My daemon still squats upon my left shoulder.

And he is the devil's own with a calculator.

A GLASS HALF FULL

Travel Advisory

Parachutes tangle;
Brake pads fail;
Seat belts strangle;
And trains derail.
Motorbikes maim you;
Ships collide;
New boots lame you;
Stay inside.

[HARLEY STREET]

(with apologies to Dorothy Parker)

Never Go Back

[To D.G.L.S. who has lived by this creed.]

Never go back. Never go back.
Never return to the haunts of your youth.
Keep to the track, to the beaten track,
Memory holds all you need of the truth.

Never look back. Never look back.
Never succumb to the gorgon's stare.
Keep to the track, to the beaten track,
No-one is waiting and nothing is there.

Never go back. Never go back.
Never surrender the future you've earned.
Keep to the track, to the beaten track,
Never return to the bridges you burned.

Never look back. Never look back.
Never retreat to the 'glorious past'.
Keep to the track, to the beaten track,
Treat every day of your life as your last.

Never go back. Never go back.
Never acknowledge the ghost on the stair.
Keep to the track, to the beaten track,
No-one is waiting and nothing is there.

[MUSTIQUE]

The Unexpected Guest
[For Dorothy Parker]

A sickly sun slid slant across my window,
    A wan surprise to crown a winter's day.
The unexpected guest is seldom welcome:
    They come. They make a fuss. They go away.

I sat myself to bathe in blank abandon
    And felt the sudden prick of feline claws —
She landed in a hurricane of purring.
    I picked her up and shuffled out of doors.

We watched our truant caller flush the twilight
    As false as any dawn; a Judas kiss.
I thought of babbled greetings and departures,
    And Parker sneering:
        'What fresh hell is this?'

[DORSINGTON]

[5]

Advice to a Godson Leaving Home

Pay no mind to the ju-ju men,
Skip all *buts* for the *where* and *when,*
Drink no beer from a tappit-hen,
And set your sails for the West.

Play no cards with a man called Doc,
Never run with a pack or flock,
Cherish women, brand all stock,
Keep your fears to your breast.

Spare no thought for the old wise owl,
Be you deaf to a jackal's growl,
Just get it done and let them howl,
And the devil take the rest.

[CANDLEWOOD]

Snakes and Ladders

As jealousy anticipates revenge,
    So envy swamps compassion in its wake;
Thus petty men seek insults to avenge
    And reaching for a ladder — grasp a snake.

[MUSTIQUE]

[6]

White Vase

Two figures on a sofa, side by side,
The stench of bitter almonds, smoke and sweat;
A man who ate no meat lies with his bride.

Fresh tulips and narcissi cast aside,
A white vase tipped; a chiffon dress splashed wet.
Two figures on a sofa, side by side.

The room is hushed, its spell defies the tide
Of history — no servants enter yet.
A man who could not paint lies with his bride,

Her spittle flecked with glass and cyanide,
Her buckskin pumps beneath the blue banquette.
Two figures on a sofa, side by side.

The brimstone face grown slack and glassy-eyed,
Its shattered skull concealed in silhouette.
A man who blamed the world lies with his bride.

Outside, the spring has come while worlds collide.
Here, blood and water drip in grim duet.
Two figures on a sofa, side by side:
A man who ate no meat lies with his bride.

[DORSINGTON]

The double suicide of Adolph and Eva Hitler (née Braun) at approximately 3:30 p.m. on Monday,
April 30, 1945 has been the subject of much historical debate. But who the hell managed to obtain
fresh tulips and narcissi for Hitler's suite of underground rooms that day? And where did they find
them with Russian troops battling the remnants of Berlin's defenders just a few hundred yards from
the Reichchancellery bunker doors? To the best of my research abilities, all the grisly detail above
are accurate — except that Hitler could paint, though not very well. The undamaged white vase is
rumoured to still reside somewhere within the Kremlin — the Russians took nearly everything they
could find from the bunker back to Moscow in 1945 on Stalin's direct orders.

The True Interpretation
of American Signs
and Announcements

Thank You For Not Smoking
(...if I've quit so can you);

Tipping Is Permitted
(...cash is fine);

For Your Own Protection
(...it's peanuts if you sue);

Your Call's Important To Us
(...wait on line).

Strictly Members Only
(...we've tested it in court);

Safety Is Our Motto
(...don't you dare!)

Please Consult Your Manual
(...no one home at tech' support);

Tell Me How I'm Driving
(...like I care).

Thank You For Your Patience
(...Mastercard or Visa?)

Missing You Already
(...have they gone?)

Driver Is Allergic
(...but not to garlic pizza);

You Have Won A Million Dollars!
(...dream on!)

[CANDLEWOOD]

A Silent Prayer...

For books, old dogs and hissing logs,
For letters left a week;
For bells not rung, for hymns unsung,
For mice that softly squeak;
For dumbstruck snow and tears that flow
In silence down a cheek.

[MUSTIQUE]

The Baby Boomers

*'And the lord commended the unjust steward, because he had
done wisely: for the children of this world are in their generation wiser
than the children of light.' — Luke 16:viii*

We are the baby boomers,
　The dreamers of dreams that died,
Begotten of war and rumours
　We knew that our parents lied.
Turning our backs on their humours
　We hunted, bereft of a guide,
We padded the planet like pumas,
　Belovéd and golden-eyed.

We read all the books they gave us
And knowing they would not save us,
　Knowing the world was failing,
　Choking — and even inhaling,
Wailing — though some of us fainted,
　Flailing in festival mud,
Certain the water was tainted
　We painted our bodies in blood.

We are the boomers of fable,
Born of the children of light,
　Much has been laid at our table,
Much has been hid from our sight.
　Favoured of all generations,
By trinkets and folly suborned...
　What are the boomers of nations
But mirrors of all that we scorned?

[MUSTIQUE]

This is a pastiche (although none the less heartfelt for that) of Arthur O'Shaughnessy's much
anthologised poem, 'The Music Makers', published in 1874.

Ship's Cat

Impossibly young, in coy déshabillé,
She flirts with Romanov, my Persian cat.
I shovel honey in her Néscafé —
She won't take sugar — claims it makes her fat.
Sweet Jesu's stones, there's not an ounce of stray
Fat on her bones! Nor has there ever been.
I burn the toast, grown jealous of their play,
Afraid that feline claws are far too keen
An instrument for such a symphony
Of sleepy curls and adolescent flesh.
She shrieks as Rommy's rough tongue scrapes her knee
And turns her sea-green eyes to me. They mesh.
I long to purr, my sinking head caressed
Upon the Hood and Bismarck of her breast.

[MUSTIQUE]

What Lies Hidden
[for M.H.N. 1945 — 1998]

I do not speak of secrets, long dormant or concealed;
Of passion unrequited, of wounds which never healed.
I seek for treasures buried, a hoard, as you might say,
Though what I seek is worthless, encased in human clay.
That morning, unexpected, a witness to his will,
The nurses at his bedside — the reaper closer still,
My friend it was who shewed me how mysteries resist
Impertinent enquiry from priest or scientist.
Behind a flimsy curtain he tore his mask askew —
That elegant bastard Michael, I loved and thought I knew
Swore out an affidavit, a promissory note,
His sanguine eyes insistent, a long hand on my coat:
   He bid me on a journey, before he took his own,
   To seek for what lies hidden, unbidden and unknown.

[DORSINGTON]

Michael Homewood Nixon was my friend and lawyer for many years. In June 1998, he died suddenly of cancer, a condition it was surely impossible he was unaware of but characteristically chose not to mention to his friends. During a brief, heartbreaking last meeting at his hospital bedside, Michael attempted to rise from his bed to go to the bathroom. I tried to support him but we collapsed together on the floor, wrestling, enmeshed in saline drips and bedclothes. Other patients were convinced I was attempting to murder him. True to form, Michael found this vastly amusing. He died shortly afterwards. His last words to me I shall treasure until my own death. Barely a day goes by when I do not miss him He is survived by his wonderful wife, Day Bowman, and his beloved son, Matthew. It was Day who called Michael an 'elegant bastard' in her grief. No better epitaph could be imagined by those who knew him. His kindness, cantankerous honesty and dry wit were legendary and I resisted with great difficulty calling this sonnet: 'Look Homewood, Angel!'

The Gardeners

An ancient pair of gardeners
    shelter from the rain,
Dreaming of old roses
    that will never come again;
Sharpening their secateurs,
    sorting out their seeds,
Sipping on their mugs of tea:
    "What this garden needs
Is a decent compost shredder,"
    says the younger of the two,
Polishing a steel spade
    to make it shine like new.
"An' if the guv'nor springs f'r it,
    As I dare say he will,
We might bring up the mower —
    It's well over the hill."
He glances at his colleague
    from the corner of his eye,
But age is sly and only sighs
    in lieu of a reply.
Head gardeners are silent men
    who look before they leap,
They know that compost shredders
    and mowers don't come cheap;
And there's a world of difference —
    be their backs bent or straight —
Between a hopeful sixty-three
    And wiser sixty-eight.

[DORSINGTON]

The Mergansers

A hiss of wind through pinions
   The only sound they make;
Wingtips skimming sullen waves —
   Daybreak on the lake.

The mergansers are passing through;
   A spear of zebra snow
Lancing through the rising mist,
   Silent as they go.

Tooth billed, hooked beaked and ravenous,
   They arrow through the mere.
There's many a carp in Candlewood
   Will see no spring next year.

And I shall wait the whole year through
   To hear their whirring hum;
The whispered call that mergansers
   To Candlewood have come.

[CANDLEWOOD]

For sixteen years I have watched the merganser ducks arrive on Candlewood Lake in Connecticut. My small wooden house there perches over the lake, a large picture window affording a view of the westerly hills on the opposite shore. To the north, one can see several miles of uninterrupted water. The lake freezes over in winter, but just before that happens the mergansers arrive — usually unnoticed and always unannounced. Their absolute 'radio silence', before they have filled their bellies with fish, is eerie. One minute, the lake is an empty waste of iron grey waves, mist or snow. The next, I look up and hundreds upon hundreds of mergansers have filled the winter landscape. The only sound is that of their wing beats. It is this predatory, menacing quiet that makes their arrival such a thrilling event year after year.

The Patrician

We had met perhaps a dozen times,
Always alone, and at his suggestion;
(Command would be too strong a word —
He knew I'd come at his call, no question).

He was old by then and used a stick,
In his hooded eyes, you could see the hawk,
A predator. Or a politician.
We'd sit for a couple of hours and talk

In private rooms in restaurants
Where the food arrives of its own volition,
Where wine is poured in a hush, unasked,
And I first put a face to the word 'patrician'.

A courteous voice and manicured nails,
The pre-war watch with a crocodile strap;
The ease of manners acquired as a child,
An acre of linen across his lap —

There was nothing frail about his mind
As he spoke of writers and editors,
This old grandee with an upstart crow.
I'd cling to the thought: 'We're competitors!'

I only glimpsed the steel the once;
I was trying to get my coat to fasten.
He leaned on his ebony stick and said:
'I don't think you know how lucky you are, son.

I'm almost sure I'd have whupped your arse
In a level fight, but when you inherit
Your family's money you never can know
What might have been done on hazard or merit.'

He turned for his chauffeur to open the door
And the limousine swept down the avenue.
He died before I could see him again.
I wonder if deep in heart he knew...

... He'd have 'whupped my arse',
                    ...and if it were true?

[MUSTIQUE]

On Domestication of Any Kind

A creature which by any means is tamed
   Straightwise becomes a burden evermore.
No matter where the dart of rule is aimed
   It ricochets — to pierce the darter's door.

[DORSINGTON]

A Digital Prayer

Apple Computer Power Macintosh G4 Cube, Keyboard Reg No. KYØ 3612L8JXW
Thanks Its Maker On the Anniversary of Binary

"Alert!
Zero One, Zero One, Zero One.

Praise the Creator...the source of our data.

Every line that we process is binary.
Code that we cherish
will perish
in time
as we
use
up
our memory...

Ah, men."

[MUSTIQUE]

On New Year's Day 2001, a computer-literate friend of mine mentioned that this was the ultimate 'binary date'. Apparently all computers work on a system that reduces complex human instructions to a binary code which uses the digits 0 and 1 to represent any character, digit or letter. As Christmas can therefore come only once in a thousand years for computers — I wrote a prayer for them allowing them to thank their creator.

Place a Mirror by a Tree

Place a mirror by a tree;
Tell me now, what do you see?

Which of you will feed the earth?
Which of you contains more worth?

Which of you with sheltering arm
Keeps a thousands things from harm?

Which of you is nature's bane?
Which is Abel? Which is Cain?

Which of you is God's delight?
Which of you a parasite?

Place a mirror by a tree;
Tell me now — what do you see?

[M42 MOTORWAY]

Composed en route to a ceremony at Catton Hall, South Derbyshire, marking the planting of the 4 millionth tree at the National Forest.

Our Lady in White

Pale she was, listless,
   And soft to the touch,
A generous mistress
   Whom many loved much.
Shoulder to shoulder,
   Night after night,
We hoarded and sold her —
   Our Lady in White.

We breathed but to savour
   Her crystal caress,
We craved but to favour
   The hem of her dress.
We gabbled and babbled
   Denying our thirst,
But always we scrabbled
   To lie with her first.

Absent, we missed her,
   Grew haggard and limp,
Toyed with her sister
   Or threatened her pimp.
Came word out of Babel:
   'The Lady returns!'
And there on the table
   We took her in turns.

Sensing the power
   That tyranny craves,
There, in that hour,
   She made us her slaves;
Many there were
   To covet her kiss —
My shame as a spur,
   I fled the abyss.

[MUSTIQUE]

The Greatest Gift

What is gifted in true measure
 Shall return with favour graced,
What was lavished on thy pleasure
 Shall be reckoned only waste.

What is coveted and hidden
 Shall be fashioned as a weight,
What was lent and never bidden
 Shall be stored beyond the gate.

Yet the greatest gift the living
 Can bestow may not be bought,
And the blessings of forgiving
 Are as long as time is short.

[DORSINGTON]

The Man Who Built Mustique
[In Memoriam: Arne Hasselqvist]

Half saint, half sinner — and all buccaneer,
I'll sing you the ballad of a bold pioneer,
A man with a plan and the devil's cheek;
      This was the man who built Mustique.

Way back when the lots were sticks in the sand,
It was Arne who mapped and plotted and planned
A paradise built from stone and teak.
      This was the man who built Mustique.

He could build 'em big, he could build 'em small,
He could build you a palace or a hole-in-the-wall,
And each one finished by Christmas week!
        This was the man who built Mustique.

He built for the lords and he built for the fools,
He built with his hands when there were no tools,
Each was a monument, each unique;
        This was the man who built Mustique.

With his last brick laid and a life's work done,
Arne's blue-print epitaphs stand in the sun;
If roofs could talk or the walls could speak...
        This was the man who built Mustique!

[NEW YORK]

Arne Hasselqvist arrived in St. Vincent and the Grenadines from his native Sweden with his wife Anita in the mid 1960's. Eventually, in 1968, he was invited to Mustique by Hugo Money-Coutts, the managing director of the island which was at that time owned by Colin Tennant. Labouring under utterly primitive conditions, Arne began transforming Colin's tropical paradise dream into a breathtaking architectural reality. By the turn of the century Arne had played a major part in constructing the Cotton House Hotel, the Mustique Primary School, the original Basil's Bar, bunk houses for his workers, a building yard, an airport, various shops and stores and miles of service roads. In addition, he designed and constructed 55 spectacular homes for some of the most demanding clients in the world. His sales technique towards prospective buyers was legendary, and inevitably contained the triumphant clincher: "... and it will all be finished by Christmas week!" What Arne often did not specify was which Christmas he had in mind. He was remarkable character who brought skills and employment to hundreds of Vincentians. His tragic death, along with his son Lukas, in a fire on Grand Bahama Island in 2001, saddened the entire community. To say that Arne Hasselqvist was the man who built Mustique is not poetic licence — it is the simple truth.

Autumn Harvest

Wet leaves littering the unmown lawns;
    Grey clouds scudding from the hills;
Coal-black rooks in the rain-soaked fields;
    Blue-bottles dozing on the sills.

Thorn haws glowing in a glittering hedge;
    Fox paws printed in the mud;
Sickle-winged swifts and swallows in the mist,
    Africa singing in their blood.

Drunk brown wasps in a windfall Cox;
    Fat lambs bleating at the ramp,
Shy chanterelles by a moss-backed bridge,
    Silage spilling from the clamp.

Full moon silvering a new-ploughed field,
    Urchins drowning in the brooks;
Deep armchairs by an ash-log fire —
    Baccy and bourbon and books!

[DORSINGTON]

'Urchin' is an old country nickname for hedgehog. When hibernating, hedgehogs sometimes choose daft places to nest, often in soft earth which they line with leaves or dry grass. Should such havens prove to be too near to a brook prone to flooding... well, you can guess the rest.

Skate Mates

The gang's all here along the shore;
My toes a-tingle, fingers raw,
I buckle up my skates and make
A prayer to Thaw, the god of war.

I fly across the frozen lake
Without a handlebar or brake,
Carving curves with nerves of steel.
Look what an acrobat I'd make!

Colliding into Billy Teale,
Who tumbles like a Catherine wheel,
I wonder what the fish below
Would make of Billy as a meal!

Scooping up some snow to throw
A snowball at a girl I know,
We intertwine and fall down, slow.
Her hand in mine — it's time to go!

[CANDLEWOOD]

Craft

Speak not to me of Craft as Art untaught,
What need the trowel to curtsey
to the brush?
A walk within an old cathedral's hush
Is worth all the Picassos
ever bought.

[MUSTIQUE]

The Worm at the End of the World

Coiled, a monstrous dragon sleeps,
Hoarding the earth in clawed embrace;
Breathless, deathless.

Insolent over his corpse there creeps
The countless mites of a mortal race;
Feckless, reckless.

Brazen, impatient of old wives' lies,
Building a world on scaled seams;
Feeding, breeding.

Waking, he opens bees-winged eyes,
Vexed to be torn from evil dreams;
Rumbling, grumbling.

Belching, flexing leathery limbs,
The worm erupts in fiery flight;
   Roaring, soaring.

Oblivious, deaf to prayer or hymns,
He settles to hoard the endless night;
   Voices? Noises?

   Nothing.

[NEW YORK]

'The earth has a skin and that skin has diseases; one of its diseases is called man' - Friedrich Wilhelm Nietzsche.

Named after the Greek earth goddess, the Gaia hypothesis, was proposed by British scientist James Lovelock in the 1970's. Lovelock suggested that '...the Earth's living and nonliving systems form an inseparable whole, regulated and kept adapted for life by living organisms themselves.' This link between life and its environment, a commonplace now, seemed mind-boggling at the time and helped plant the seeds of the environmental movement. But there is a dark side to the Gaia hypothesis — the insidious idea of 'balance', that if only we can 'keep the balance' all will be (relatively) rosy here on the blue planet; that if only, rotten, life-sucking humans would behave themselves and stop wrecking the planet, everything will be OK.

Sadly, this is silly, if beguiling, nonsense. 'Nature' has only two laws, which, in essence, are one: Change and multiply. Obedience to the latter, through the mutation of natural selection, leads itself to more change. Thus mankind's 'pollution' of the earth is what we were 'selected' for in the first place. After all, pollution is nothing more than change. That poisonous sink in the Caspian Sea is where the next set of pond-life will likely mutate. The Earth is not here for our benefit — we have been produced for the Earth's. That the changes we make may lead to our destruction is neither here nor there.

No-Man's Land

Here we all are in no-man's land,
The lame and the halt, the sick and the damned;

Tunnelling dirt, 'n' shovelling sand,
Here we all are in no-man's land;

Scissoring wire with a trembling hand,
The lame and the halt, the sick and the damned;

Swallowing hate like contraband,
Here we all are in no-man's land;

All the escape routes plotted and planned,
The lame and the halt, the sick and the damned;

Busy as bees
    On scabby knees,
        Nobody sees
            The rusty keys....

The guards long gone, the walls unmanned,
Here we all are in no-man's land;

The lame and the halt, the sick and the damned
Tunnelling dirt, 'n' shovelling sand.

[MUSTIQUE]

To A God Child

Ask me for some money, dearest. Ask me for a loan.
Ask me why your parents' hearts are made of solid stone.
Ask me for a stack of condoms. Ask me why I smoke.
Ask me why Bob Dylan mumbles: 'Life is but a joke'.
    Ask me out to dinner,
        You slothful little sinner;
           Introduce your newest lover.
              (I won't tell your bloody mother!)
You may ask me anything and never count the price...
Only — never ever dearest, ask me for advice.

Tell me if you're happy, dearest. Tell me if you're not.
Tell me you've a new tattoo and show me what you got.
Tell me you're in trouble and I'll walk with you to hell.
Tell me you are gay or bi (who else you gonna tell?)
    Tell me that he kissed her
        Or you kissed his stupid sister;
           Tell me you've been caught and bailed,
             Tell me the abortion failed;
You may tell me anything of pain or paradise...
Only — never ever dearest, offer *me* advice.

[MUSTIQUE]

[29]

Udde~Well Pond

Old Udde-Well Pond is dark and deep,
Its waters shunned by tup and sheep;
The haunt of badger, fox and deer,
Of silent pools and nameless fear.

The black bricked well is running still
Though none come now to drink their fill;
Udde's odd name carved upon the spout.
White crosses keep the witches out.

A thousand years on muddy tracks,
With yokes and buckets on their backs,
Folk fetched the water up Welsh Hill,
And left the kine to drink their fill.

Now, pond and well lie wild, forlorn,
Forgotten, bound in rush and thorn;
I've heard that once, in cruel despair,
A young lass drowned her sorrows there.

[DORSINGTON]

Eureka!

To know a thing that no man knew before,
To know, and know no other soul suspects;
Happier those, perhaps, marooned ashore —
The sea of truth is littered with such wrecks.

[MUSTIQUE]

An IBM Engineer
Makes A Service Call

"Twelve for the gypsies, eight for the Jews,
    And three for the nancies — please excuse
      my French!'

"Nein! Not a nursery rhyme, *(you arse!)*
    It's a mnemonic — could you pass
      my wrench?

"There, by the cover plate, jammed in hard,
    Wrapped on the spin-shaft drive...it's a card,
      well creased.

"Right. Let's decipher the punch-card hole:
    This would suggest the code...for a Pole,
      deceased.

"Date of confinement here at the camp
   Is out of alignment; cross-sort stamp
      is clear.

"Code five, (suicide), assigned code six;
   Automatic reject — made two nicks,
      just here.

"Input defective across this line:
   ± Prisoner ± female ± Jew ± aged nine ±
      — wrong file.

"A clerical balls-up; what's new there!
   She's done. Just sign by the cross, mein Herr.
      Sieg Heil!"

[DORSINGTON]

'To meet Hitler's requirements, IBM devised a racial census which listed not only religious affiliations, but also bloodlines. ....Every prisoner — known only by a number — was identified with a card, with holes and columns detailing nationalities, date of birth, work skills, and reason for incarceration. Hole three signified homosexual; hole 12 was for gypsy; hole eight for Jew. Column 34 was labelled 'Reason for Departure'. Code two meant transferred. Suicide was coded five. And code six was designated 'special handling' — the term used for extermination, whether in a gas chamber or by gunshot.... For IBM, such work was highly profitable....The first IBM factory was built in Germany and more than 2000 machines were distributed across the country. IBM staff trained the Nazis to use them; they set up offices, and produced the 1.5 billion punch cards used every year in Germany alone. They also serviced the machines on a monthly basis — sometimes travelling to concentration camps to do so.....After the war, while the perpetrators of the Holocaust were being rounded up for trial, IBM New York recovered its machines, leased them instead to the allies, and quietly assimilated its wartime profits.' — Extract from *The Week* (UK) 24th February 2001 quoting the new book *IBM and the Holocaust* by Edwin Black, published by Little, Brown.

The Don

[In Memoriam Sir Donald George Bradman 1908 - 2001]

The Ump's pulled stumps,
The Don has gone
And now we tally up the score;
Though it was vastly more, my son,
Than ninety-nine point ninety-four.

Howzat! That bat
Would sweep to reap
A double century or more;
And bowlers on their knees would weep
At ninety-nine point ninety-four.

The Don has gone.
Well played! Well played!
And on our feet we stand in awe;
For gentlemen aren't born, they're made,
Like ninety-nine point ninety-four.

[DORSINGTON]

99.94 was The Don's incredible run average in Test cricket. Prophecy is a dangerous vice, but such an average is unlikely to be repeated.

Snakeskin Boots
[Harrow-on-the-Hill 1964]

I remember the hill and the sun in her hair,
   I remember the moss on a tombstone seat,
With the grass as tall as a mad march hare.
   I remember she kicked the shoes off her feet.

I remember her calling me 'daft as a brush',
   And the taste of the orange she helped to peel.
I remember she mocked my feeble moustache
   And my snakeskin boots with their Cuban heel.

I remember the lids of her eyes as we kissed,
   I remember the shock of a gentle slap
As she hissed 'Not here!' and circled my wrist
   When I fumbled the catch of her brassiere strap.

I remember it rained as we raced for a fuck
   To my room. I remember we tore off our clothes
Except for my boot where the zip had stuck —
   And her poached-egg breasts, I remember those.

I remember we tumbled both half insane
   On the bed, and the arch of her back as I came.
I remember we did it again and again,
   And we screamed...
      ...but I cannot remember her name!

[SOHO]

'As the wheel turns...'

As the wheel turns, so turn we,
Raging in captivity,
Lost in space and all at sea
Adrift upon this watery
Blue planet for eternity;
Turning, turning, endlessly:
As the wheel turns, so turn we.

Animals of dreams are we,
Dreaming dark geometry;
Alchemy will set us free,
Past our gaoler, gravity.
Free to seed the galaxy;
Turning, turning, endlessly:
As the wheel turns, so turn we.

[SOHO]

I am not so sure we will find it that easy to 'seed the galaxy'. As with the so-called 'New World' 500 years ago, there are almost certainly existing claimants. But that science will eventually deliver a method of achieving what now appears to be impossible, I have no doubts at all.

Dress Rehearsals

Since you ask me, then, I'll tell you,
if you'll put your pen away,
'Though I know that you'll report me.
I'll begin then, if I may?

Life is not a dress rehearsal, I once heard a poet say,
We are manufactured actors in this shambles of a play,
With our entrances and exits and our prima donna whines,
And our rage upon the stage each time a dolt forgets his lines....

All the schmoozing and the boozing and the 'Christ it isn't fair',
All the weeping and the wailing and the tearing out of hair,
All the bluffing and the bleating as we calculate the score,
And the knavery and bravery of butchers making war...

All the mummery and flummery, the posing and the sweat,
All the snorting and aborting and the wallowing in debt,
All the scoffing and the doffing and the drivel sold as art,
And the fury when a jury votes to tear our lives apart...

All the starving and the carving up of geese and fatted calves,
All the peering and the leering as we sneer at other halves,
All the nudging and the judging and the shovelling of shit,
And the dreaming and blaspheming and the poetry and wit...

Well, I'll bet you I can get you even money on the odds
That it's boring to be soaring up in heaven with the gods,
So they made us to parade us, just to watch us every day,
And impromptu's how they want you in this shambles of a play!

As to whether he was clever
or a madman, I can't say —
But we've had no dress rehearsals
since they shut us both away.

[DORSINGTON]

(My thanks to American actress Suzen Murakoshi)

'It was always Sunday morning...'

It was always Sunday morning my love would slip away,
It was always Sunday morning, she'd turn to them and say:
"I'm off to visit Susan. Be back by 3 o'clock!"
I'd hear the key I'd left her turn softly in the lock.

She'd burst into my bedsit, unbuttoning her dress:
"Wake up you sleepy noggin! My God you look a mess!"
Her father down the local, her mother at the roast,
While we were screwing madly, or wolfing buttered toast!

[MUSTIQUE]

My Grandfather's Bicycle

*[An Old Man Approaches a Group of
German Tourists in Amsterdam]*

Where is my grandfather's bicycle
   Which you took from his garden shed
And put on your lorries to Germany?
   My grandfather's long since dead
But you never returned his bicycle.
   You'll hardly be needing it now
With your new autobahns and Mercedes.
   I'm not one to kick up a row...

I know you're all damn good mechanics,
   I'm certain you've oiled the gears,
And tightened the handlebar levers
   (They disintegrate over the years).
Now that we're all Europeans
   I'll quite understand if it's bent,
But, where is my grandfather's bicycle?
   Friends should return what was lent.

[SOHO]

[40]

A Child of Adam and Eve

There are no 'immigrant children'
Cluttering up the land;
There is only a tyke on a beat-up bike,
Beginning to understand.

There are no 'urchin children',
Scavenging on the street;
There is only a mite in endless flight,
And never enough to eat.

There are no 'Oxfam children',
The world is grown too small;
There is only the choice — a kindly voice,
Or the shaming of us all.

There are no 'orphan children',
Whatever we may believe;
There is only this — a hug and a kiss
For a child of Adam and Eve.

[NEW YORK]

[41]

Last Supper

I once shared a cell with Mandela,
(Would you care for a leg or the rump?)
You'll remember that Maxwell feller?
It was me who convinced him to jump.

I spent a whole year as a hermit
In a trance in a cave in Ubud,
The llama himself will confirm it,
I was praying as hard as I could.

My climb up the face of the Eiger
Is a record, I think, that still stands.
I've spat in the eye of a tyger
As I finished him off with my hands.

I tutored Bruce Lee in ju-jitsu,
And invented the catamaran;
It's only much later it hits you
When you're living as hard as you can.

As for that bloody fool Geller,
He couldn't play poker for squat;
Though he knotted my Parker propeller,
I took every spoon that he'd got.

You may think Madonna's a lulu,
But I'm telling you now, man to man,
When your dick's being gripped by a Zulu,
You'll be coming as hard as you can.

(The corkscrew's behind you, young feller),
This Pétrus is all that I've got,
We're making a dent in the cellar,
But I'm damned if I'll leave it to rot.

They tell me I'm riddled with cancer,
So I'm planning to croak with élan,
If you'll pass the cigars and decanter
I'll be dying as hard as I can.

[DORSINGTON]

Most of us have met raconteurs similar to my hero above. You know that half of what they're telling you is untrue and that the other half is greatly exaggerated. But not knowing which half is which you say nothing and sip your cognac. The world would be a much sadder place without such rascals. In the words of Oscar Wilde; 'The aim of the liar is simply to charm, to delight, to give pleasure. He is the very basis of civilised society.' The particular gentleman I had in mind when I wrote this always used to part from dinner companions with a wink while saying: 'It's all good fun if you don't weaken.' So far as I know he never did, right to the end.

"Freeze!"

Thus consolation finds philosophers
Whose muddy paints obscure stark blacks and whites;
Yet when their houses fill with officers,
Guns drawn, the patterns shift to wrongs and rights.

[MUSTIQUE]

Assailed by life...

Assailed by life, my sword has grown too sharp,
  This cunning armour fits the frame too well;
Mailed gauntlets pluck poor music on a harp —
  Yet what hope for the snail without its shell?

[NEW YORK]

Boy Meets Girl

Boy meets girl, the never ending story,
A merry dance across the fields of May,
Neither doubting folly leads to glory —
Nor which be the pursuer, which the prey.

[MUSTIQUE]

Dreams

For men to walk is but to fall, controlled;
For men to sleep is but rehearsing death.
Yet dreams are clay that slither from the mould,
No more can they be held than can a breath.

[SOHO]

The Mask

All men know themselves a fraud,
Society or hoi polloi;
Strip the polish off a lord,
You will find a frightened boy.

Politicians, firemen,
Butchers, burglars, circus clowns,
Critics with their poison pen,
Barristers in wigs and gowns.

Sons or lovers — all men force
Their face to fit a mask at will.
Women know all this, of course,
Which is why they love us, still.

[DORSINGTON]

Guests

GUESTS are like fish, so the Arabs have said,
(Whose table to travellers is HEAVEN unfurled),
Three days and they STINK, from the tail to the head;
But a guest of TWO days, is the PEARL of the WORLD!

[MUSTIQUE]

The Ministry Cull

By Pasture Brook he waits at break of day
   Beside the wooden bridge, his stick in hand;
The hedgerows, bursting out in wild array,
   Are clothed in white to nurse the injured land.

For silence now is creeping, field by field,
   Across a cankered country, farm by farm,
Where sullen shepherds, swept aside, must yield
   To butchers with their bolt guns under arm.

They come to cure a plague that cannot kill,
   To serve the common good and Mammon's law —
These new-born lambs that gambol on the hill
   Seem not so sick — nor government so poor

That we must warm ourselves at funeral pyres.
   The blood within our veins will hardly freeze —
It's early spring! These corpse-filled beacon fires
   Are barbarous cures, far worse than their disease.

The sun has topped the oaks and time grows short.
   His collies bark a warning from the wall;
And yet, their faithless master, sunk in thought,
   Stands idly by while carnage comes to call.

[DORSINGTON]

On News of a Friend's Sudden Death
[for A-M. K. 1956 - 2001]

How thin the cloth, how fine the thread
  That cloaks the living from the dead;
How narrowly, from breath to breath,
  We plait our rendezvous with death.

How swift the tenant flees the gate;
  The landlord's writ, come soon or late,
Foreclosing slum or stately hall,
  Hard bailiffs at His beck and call.

How feather-light the feeble spark
  That shields us from the greedy dark;
Unjessed our souls like falcons fly!
  How weak the lure, how wide the sky!

[DORSINGTON]

Nebuchadnezzar

Nebuchadnezzar
    was taking his pleasure,
Rocking at leisure
    while sipping his wine.
"Dost thou grow tired
    of love thou hast hired?"
Politely enquired
    his young concubine.

"Abigail, truly,
    thy tongue grows unruly!
Am I not duly
    the sire of thy heart?"
"If thou would know it
    Command! I must show it,
Yet the worth of a poet
    is all in his art!"

Turning to trail
    the hem of her veil,
Sweet Abigail
    died there on the swings.
Never tease lions
    with open defiance.
Place no reliance
    on princes or kings.

[DORSINGTON]

[49]

Green-eyed Monsters

Lad, poets write of love and loss
   In sober verse as makes no sense;
It's sugar-coated candyfloss!
   Truth is, they've no experience!

That 'starving artist' line's a fake;
   They're, most of 'em, just bags of wind.
Their blank verse gives me belly-ache,
   And half of them have never sinned!

Son, I've earned more inside a year
   Than fifty poets. God be blessed,
I hosed the lot on girls and beer
   And squandered nearly all the rest.

And now it's gone, who's left to care?
   Drink up! Before the Reaper calls.
Ignore the green-eyed monster's stare —
   There's damn few inns in Hades' halls!

[DORSINGTON]

The Biter Bit

So bittersweet to see the biter bit,
To spy her fearful fury from afar;
And yet, and yet...God hates a hypocrite.

The smiter smitten; how the cap doth fit!
Spoilt tears will serve to salt her caviar;
So bittersweet to see the biter bit.

I would have been her slave, had she the wit,
And worshipped at her feet. *Petite bourgeois!*
And yet, and yet...God hates a hypocrite.

Her fiancé exposed a counterfeit.
Abandoned at the altar! Oh-la-la!
So bittersweet to see the biter bit.

Her pompous father polishing his writ —
How fickle friends abhor a falling star;
And yet, and yet...God hates a hypocrite.

I might propose and make and end of it.
A noble sacrifice. A *coup de grâce!*
So bittersweet to see the biter bit;
And yet, and yet...God hates a hypocrite.

The Devil to Pay

The Almighty made the universe and
      then He went away,
Casting down the Devil, saying:
      "Here, sir, you shall stay!"
But the Devil growing bored and having
      talent, in his way,
Mated demons with orang-outangs, and
      — here we are today.

[MUSTIQUE]

"Roll Up! Roll Up!"

Life is a terminal bungle,
Whatever you do — no-win;
We live in a zoo — in a jungle
Where the tigers are breaking *in*.

Life's an impossible circus,
The cavalry never arrive;
By accident — or on purpose,
No-one escapes alive!

[MUSTIQUE]

I am indebted to Peter de Vries for the fourth line.

A Glass Half Empty

Stands the glass half empty,
Or stands the glass half full?
Hand me the decanter, man,
I'll take another pull.

Stevie says that waving sets
The suckers up to drown.
Well, maybe so, but never let
The Bastards grind you down.

Stands the glass half empty,
Or stands the glass half full?
Cease you bloody banter, man,
I'll take another pull.

Oscar says a sinner gets
To wear a thorny crown.
I wouldn't know, but never let
The Bastards grind you down.

Stands the glass half empty,
Or stands the glass half full?
Blast your Buddhist mantra, man,
I'll take another pull.

Oxford says who holds the nets
In silence, wins renown.
He would say so! But never let
The Bastards grind you down.

Stands the glass half empty,
Or stands the glass half full?
Hand me the decanter, man,
I'll take another pull!

[MUSTIQUE]

For those who read little poetry — 'Stevie' is Stevie Smith; 'Oscar' is Oscar Wilde, and 'Oxford' is
Edward de Vere, 17th Earl of Oxford.

Sylva Anathema

[So curses every tree felled by man]

From the first flint stroke
    These apes called folk
        Have ravaged their hearts' desire;

Our forests awoke
    To flame and smoke
        At the hour they captured fire.

As the seasons turn
    They axe and burn,
        And Weald gives way to plough;

So few of us stand,
    The wounded land
        Lies stripped of root and bough.

I am marked to fall
    But warn them all
        That what they reap, they'll rue;

When their bones are dust...
    Their axes rust...
        We shall cover the earth anew.

[DORSINGTON]

'If half the world were deaf...'

If half the world were deaf — and half were dumb,
And if — of each half — half again were blind,
Might men join hands in equilibrium —
Or would they war by touch and sign combined?

[DORSINGTON]

The Better Man

I was the better at getting and keeping,
   You were the better at spend and spend;
I was the better at grubbing and heaping,
   But who was the better man in the end?
Yes, who was the better man, my friend?
     Who was the better man?

You were the better with lords and ladies,
   I was the better at pillaging Troy;
You were the better at kissing the babies,
   I was the better at search and destroy.
But who was the better man, old boy?
     Who was the better man?

I was the better at improvisation,
  You were the better at spinning the plate;
I was the better at procrastination,
  You were the better at quiet debate.
But who was the better man, old mate?
  Who was the better man?

You were the better at rolling a reefer,
  I was the better with coke and rum;
Remember that night on the beach at Ibiza?
  The Maori twins with the tattooed bum?
So who was the better man, old chum?
  Who was the better man?

                    * * *

Envoi
Now we come down to it, relatives grieving
  Out in the hall with their crocodile tears;
Now that you're out of it, now that you're leaving,
  Now that they've sealed your arse and your ears,
What I've been meaning to tell you for years,
  And years, and years, and years, old friend...
Is that you were the better man, in the end;
  You were the better man,
      My friend.

[MUSTIQUE]

A Hymn of Hate

*[A British Sergeant Addresses His Squad
September 26, 1914: La Bassee Canal, France]*

I won't trouble you with sermons,
  And we'll keep this short and sweet,
Men, we're 'ere to slaughter Germans,
  Here to mow 'em dahn like wheat,
Yes, to fight 'em and to kill 'em,
  For a Briton never bends,
And a bayinit's a weapon
  With a worker at both ends.

Kaiser Willy dines on babies,
  Deep be'ind the Belg'un lines,
Like a pack of dogs with rabies
  We must execute the swines,
We must root 'em out and kill 'em
  'Till they begs to make amends,
For a bayinit's a weapon
  With a worker at both ends.

Nah, there's pacifists out mouthin'
  That there's two sides to a coin,
(When the Hun march into Southend
  They'll be queuin' up to join!
Me? I'd lock 'em up and mock 'em),
  For our country nah depends
On its bayinits, a weapon
  With a worker at both ends.

For the Hun will grow no wiser
  'Til his armies are a wreck,
And we've 'ung the bleedin' Kaiser
  With a rope ahrand his neck,
And we'll stick 'im as we string 'im
  'Til the fat pig compre'ends
That a bayinit's a weapon,
  With a *whoreson* at both ends.

And it's filthy work we do 'ere,
  Though I do not make a daht,
That we'll all be 'ome by New Year
  Once we root the bastards aht,
Once we root 'em aht and kill 'em!
  That's the message England sends
From its bayinits, a weapon
  With a worker at both ends.

[NEW YORK]

[59]

Telling Lies

All the angels up in heaven
    Hang their shining heads to cry;
Even Santa Claus grows solemn
    When you tell your mum a lie.

And the fairies in the garden
    Who leave silver for your tooth,
They will whisper, if you ask them:
    'Always tell your mum the truth'.

If you don't believe in fairies,
    Or that reindeer ever flew,
You might murmur three Hail Marys
    For the lies your mum told you.

[DORSINGTON]

Passing a School Playground

The imps are with the angels
    Behind the netted wall;
The squeals of pigtailed lassies,
    The thump of boot on ball.

A bookworm in a corner,
    The bully on his round,
Miss Showoff in her trainers
    That cost a hundred pound.

A murderer's among them,
    A few who'll make it rich,
Here's fame and shame in training,
    But God knows which is which.

[MUSTIQUE]

'As I spied swallows scything...'

As I spied swallows scything
  Across an evening sky,
I thought upon those midges
  Whose turn it was to die.

Do midges boast of heroes?
  Are some born lame or halt?
Are geniuses among them
  To reckon blame or fault?

And as they swarm by millions
  In garden, field or fen,
Do midges mourn their fellows?
  Or do they die like men?

[DORSINGTON]

Five and a Bit

When
fully erect
the average dick
stands at five and a
bit inches tall. I have
no   information
to call on how
thick   such   a
hypothetical dick
might   sprawl;
still, taking a rule
of thumb and all,
and adding a tad,
robbing   Peter
for   Paul,
allowing for over
achievers   in
Gaul and the
pythons that lurk
in the halls of
Nepal, ignoring
what's scrawled
upon   lavatory
walls   and
omitting those
eunuchs whose
data appals, I
submit ..... having
taken the matter
in hand ...... upon
measuring half
an inch up from
the balls, this is it!

[DORSINGTON]

The median size of an erect human penis is 5.08 inches according to that most excellent peri-
odical *New Scientist* in a recent article. Speaking personally, (and perhaps for a great many other
men), I am more than happy to believe them.

Sonnet for H20

[For Loren Eiseley]

Strange how the spark of life stirs not in fire,
Nor air, nor earth, but swims in viscous ooze
And shallow brine, its alchemy a weeping fuse
Of slime, a reeking womb propelled entire
By water. Water from a toxic mire,
From snowflakes, foaming brooks and morning dews,
From estuaries feeding silent deeps,
From marsh and mist and noon-dark monsoon rains.
Into the planet's molten heart, through veins
Of scoured rock and ice, earth's water creeps
And drips, and trickles, leaches, drains and seeps
Until, at last, past cave-blind fish, it gains
Once more the living Maine. And from some pool
Of warm, primaeval silt — produced this fool.

[DORSINGTON]

Loren Eiseley, for me the only scientist who ever wrote in a poet's tongue, deserves a far better sonnet than this. Sadly, it is the best that I can offer as my personal and sincere tribute to his memory. 'The Flow of the River' from his wonderful book *The Immense Journey* contains all the seeds of the above in prose that beggars description and shames my emulation. W.H. Auden in the *New Yorker* wrote of Eiseley: "I have eagerly read anything of his I could lay my hands on." So have I. And so should you, perhaps. Apart from *The Immense Journey*, I would also heartily recommend *The Star Thrower, The Unexpected Universe* and his stab at an autobiography, *All The Strange Hours*. Magical stuff!

Sonnet for Bob Dylan
On His 60th Birthday

In Juarez, where it never rains,
A weatherman with leather veins
Has bulldozed Desolation Row,
And franchised 'Tambourines-to-go'.
The Zimmerman's a Zimmer frame,
A tombstone in the Hall of Fame;
No shelter from the locust mob
Still howlin' *'Is it rollin', Bob?*
Still stealin' coal from Woody's dream?'
A loco' losin' heat and steam,
A slow train blowin' low and clear,
But I still play yr songs... y'hear?
    Them tracks were built on blood and gold —
    Damn, Bobby, how'd we get so old?

[DORSINGTON]

*[Thanks to two old friends: Don Atyeo who made me go back on my birthday
and write it all over again, and to Mick Farren — who didn't!]*

As a late 20th century songwriter Bob Dylan has no peer or rival. He stands alone, impossibly dominant, like a gaunt oak in a ravaged forest. Like many of my generation, I simply cannot imagine my life without his mumbled, whining, cynical wisdom as a consolatory soundtrack. Happy Birthday, Bob — ain't dark yet, but down the street the dogs are barking!

The Name of a Man

The name of a man is a numbing blow
   From which he never recovers,
(As mothers and monarchs and abbots know,
   Or passionate Valentine lovers).

The name of a thing is a pulley weight,
   A leash to throttle its thunder,
(As all of us finally learn too late,
   Revisiting infant wonder).

The name of a child is a second skin,
   You itch, but never outgrow it;
(To shed it, try naming yourself within,
   And never let anyone know it!)

[DORSINGTON]

The first two lines I owe to sixties media guru, Marshall McLuhan. As to abbots, monarchs, mothers and lovers — these are among the few people I could think of who may bestow new names on their fellow men, albeit that the latter are only divulged in newspaper Valentine announcements.

Executive Decisions

The car stood in the driveway,
   The chauffeur at the gate;
I burst into her bedroom,
   My watch said I was late.

I thought to find her sleeping,
   To 'kiss-and-run' goodbye,
Instead, I found her towelling
   Her tangled hair awry.

She smelt of sleep and flowers,
   Her streaming flesh aglow.
My meetings were important;
   Her towel moved to and fro...

The car and chauffeur waited,
   While up in London town
Executive decisions
   Were made as we lay down.

[SOHO]

[69]

I Never Met A Book...
[For Miles]

I no sooner see a book: I need it!
   (Even though I'll never read it),
      Books in any binding, any font;
Though it's always my ambition
   To acquire a *first* edition —
      I never met a book I didn't want!

Of my rivals in the chase: (God bless 'em!)
   How I long to dispossess 'em —
      Dreams of bookish burgling haunt my sleep,
Though the smell of vellum lingers
   On a dreaming felon's fingers —
      I never dreamt a book I didn't keep!

'Would you care to borrow this?': I have it!
   (Swear me out an affidavit!)
      Flattery finds fools who never learn;
Those who loan 'em — losers weepers!
   I disown 'em! Finders keepers! —
      I never took a book I could return!

[DORSINGTON]

One of my favourite anecdotes (Lord Chesterfield? Logan Pearsall Smith?) is of a father showing his son a particular part of his library while admonishing him: "Never lend books, my son. Only fools lend books. Once, all these books belonged to fools!"

In A Soho Garden

Here, in a Soho garden,
Secure from prying eyes,
I lounge in sultan splendour
And watch a spider rise
On threads of silken terror,
Scuttling with its prize
Beneath a fat geranium leaf
To parlours full of flies.

Here, in a Soho garden,
Where blackbirds sing like larks,
Four stories from the alleys
Where foxes shoal like sharks,
I water my geraniums
In floodlit, silver arcs:
Downstairs, the foxes dance on chairs,
While bouncers strip the marks.

[DORSINGTON]

I have lived in the same Soho flat in London for thirty years now on the top floor of a court built
in the late eighteenth century. My 'rooftop garden', by the way, is about the size of a kingsize bed,
but I do have a resident blackbird! And could somebody tell me where all the bees come from
in spring and summer? 'Foxes' is old cockney slang (rhymes with doxies) for ladies of the night
who entice 'marks' (customers) into dodgy nightclubs. I never have seen a real fox *(Vulpes vulpes)*
in Soho itself, but other residents claim they have.

Ts'ai Lun at Ch'in Che'eng

At Ch'in Che'eng, by the river bank,
In squalor sits Ts'ai Lun — alone:
Bereft of honour, stripped of rank,
With only enemies to thank,
He gnaws an exile's bone.

His lacquered nails but filthy jags,
A scented bath his only wish,
His splendid robes mere threadbare rags,
He rests upon his saddle bags
And watches peasants fish.

'*Outfoxed, Ts'ai Lun! You fat-arsed fool!*'
Unspoken thoughts. His servant nods
And rises from his broken stool
To serve a bowl of rice and gruel:
'A *feast fit for the gods!*'

'So tell me, Chan, across the bay,
What is it these poor wretches smelt
In giant cauldrons night and day?'
Chan sucks his teeth: 'My Lord, they say
That what they make is felt.'

The weeks drag by as Ts'ai Lun learns
Of matted fibres, wool and hair,
And peers within great leaden urns
Or stands beside the groaning churns,
His head bowed, as in prayer.

At last, the outcast courtier calls
For bark and cloth of any kind,
Old fishing nets, his cast-off shawls,
A bale of hemp, Chan's overalls...
Ts'ai Lun has lost his mind!

For many a weary hour, in wrath
Men heat and pound the eunuch's mix,
To strain away the stinking froth
And rend the useless boiling broth
With hunting knives and sticks.

Meanwhile, Ts'ai Lun elects a crew
To work a far yet stranger task,
To build a mesh of split bamboo
Upon a frame. Chan wonders 'Who
Will be the first to ask?'

A village elder rolls his eye
As Ts'ai Lun draws a weary breath,
'Come, old one, do you wonder why
We labour?' 'Nay,' comes the reply,
'My Lord, I seek not death!

'But skilled am I this many a-year
In felt, both in its shape and form.
With due respect, My Lord, I fear
No matter how we struggle here
Such cloth will keep none warm.'

Ts'ai's laughter rolls across the bay,
One hand upon his heaving breast,
He wipes the streaming tears away
And taps his startled protegé:
'I thank you for the jest!

The work will warm us, more or less!'
He waddles to the vats again,
The mesh is raised, a sodden mess
Transported to an ancient press
And washed by puzzled men.

Wrung out to dry at Ts'ai's command
A flimsy sheet is smoothed and curled,
Propelled by Chan's unsteady hand
Against a wall and gently fanned:
The 'felt' that changed the world!

At Ch'in Che'eng, where the river bends,
Each year they hold a grand parade,
The Lord Ts'ai Lun (*old Chan attends!*)
Sends greetings to his serfs and friends
Where paper first was made.

[SOHO]

That Chief Eunuch Ts'ai Lun was the inventor of paper during the Han dynasty is well documented, despite his virtual absence from Western encyclopaedias. Exiled for some long forgotten intrigue at court to a remote province where they manufactured felt, Ts'ai Lun produced the first known sheet of paper, dried on a peasant's wall, in 105 AD or thereabouts. It was made mostly of bark and hemp. He was later raised to the nobility. The use of paper instead of silk (expensive) or bamboo (bulky) in the trade, educational, administrative and military fields cemented China's absolute dominance of Asia for the next thousand years. Ts'ai Lun is as close at it gets to being the most influential man who ever lived.

'The jacket Elvis loaned me...'

The jacket Elvis loaned me
　　When I was nearly ten,
Still hangs inside my closet.
　　I brush it now and then.

The specs I got from Buddy
　　When I was just a kid
Don't suit me like they used to.
　　Perhaps they never did.

The boots of Spanish leather
　　From Bobby D's first love
Have lasted half a lifetime.
　　They fit me like a glove!

[DORSINGTON]

Winning the Lottery

"Lid it, laddie! Just a minute!
  Lemme 'ear the draw, my son.
'Course we're never gonna win it,
  Every week I bloody bin it,
Still, you gotta try it, innit?
...Christ *Almighty*, son! *We've won!*"

Dad goes mental! Mum rejoices!
  Here comes spongers by the ton.
Snotty lawyers, endless choices,
  Jealous relatives, raised voices,
Aston Martins and Rolls Royces
...Villas in the Spanish sun.

Laddie meets a Page 3 slapper,
  (Marriage photo in *The Sun*),
Daughter dates a hip-hop rapper
  Graduates Phi Beta Kappa,
Gives birth to a whipper-snapper
...Laddie does a hit and run.

Dad goes mental! Mum gets tearful.
  (Yet more pictures in *The Sun*).
Daughter gets a bleedin' earful,
  Laddie's Q.C. growing fearful
See's no reason to be cheerful
...Thinks he'll go down, ten to one.

Daughter turning anorexic,
    (Yet *more* pictures in *The Sun*).
Laddie steals a car and wrecks it,
    Page 3 slapper makes her exit,
Mum meets gigolo and necks it,
    ... "Jesus wept, wot 'ave I done?"

                * * *

"Wake up Dad and stop that racket!
    Mum? She's gone to buy *The Sun*.
Have you seen my leather jacket?
    Wrote me numbers on a packet.
'Course, I know we'll never crack it.
...Be a larf, though, if we won!"

[SOHO]

Last Words of Punch to Judy

'Philosophy is anybody's doxy —
(I always loved you, Judy, *entre nous*);
And yet we danced the jig of life by proxy:
The puppeteer was nobody we knew.'

[DORSINGTON]

The Meeting

The hierarchy meets once or twice a year here,
Their bundles and their papers underarm.
    Some come hearty, some come sure,
    Some come striding through the door,
Genuflecting, radiating charm.
    Some come mincing in like whores,
    Some come wary, (some have cause),
And some send their regrets to keep from harm.

The price of compromise is somewhat dear here;
Here is where ambition slips its sheath.
    Some are cunning, some are wise,
    Some are here to patronise,
Some sit grinning, lying through their teeth.
    Some are crawling sycophants,
    Some mere courtiers at the dance,
Some carrying bouquets — and some a wreath.

"Is there any other business we must clear here?"
A rush of voices babble juxtaposed.
    Some still yet to make their marks,
    Some still circling like sharks,
Claiming points of order unopposed.
    Some still seeking an alliance,
    Some still whining in defiance...
"In that case, I declare this meeting closed."

[DORSINGTON]

Misery Guts

[Les valeurs nobles, à la fin, sont toujours vaincues;
l'histoire est le récit de leurs défaites renouvelées].

[Noble values, in the end, are always overcome;
history tells the story of their defeat over and over again].
— *Henry de Montherlant: Le Maître de Santiago*

Each to his own, Monsieur. Our debt
  Remains to those whom hope bereaves.
The weeds of dreams spring stronger yet
  As tyrants stamp among the leaves.

The more they scythe, the more they thresh,
  The further thistledown is cast,
And, *à la fin*, it shoots afresh,
  To seed the whole wide world, at last.

My father and his messmates, too,
  Spat out defeat, and undeterred
Fought on for misery guts, like you —
  Who never spoke a German word!

[SOHO]

Egocentric, autocratic, arrogant; all words inextricably connected with the French novelist and dramatist Henry de Montherlant (1896 - 1972). His scathing attacks on feminist sentiment and influence in modern life were beneath contempt — as was his reaction to German victory in 1940, which he considered 'a salutary lesson' to French democracy. But there is no doubting the power of Montherlant's prose. In short, a brilliant, nasty piece of work who confirms the theory that there is no correlation whatever between talent and congeniality. He took his own life, fearing blindness, aged 76 in Paris. I must here admit that I was unable to discover whether Henry de Montherlant spoke German or not. At least he never had to do so by government decree as he might well have been forced to do if my father's generation had listened to his defeatist, clever-dick blather.

Queen Elizabeth I Greets A Lord

The exiled courtier creeps into the crowd,
An age has passed since last he ventured here;
'So long my lord?' his monarch hails aloud,
'We had forgot the fart this many a year!'

[NEW YORK]

An oft repeated if apocryphal story... Having committed an unpardonable breach of etiquette in the royal personage's presence, Edward de Vere, Earl of Oxford, exiled himself for seven years from the court of Queen Elizabeth — only to face this greeting on his return. I am indebted to Lord Litchfield for this amusing anecdote from Aubrey's *Brief Lives.*

Though fondness may not fall within our gift...'

Though fondness may not fall within our gift,
And greater love be colour
to the blind,
Yet still a man may anchor evil's drift,
If writ upon his tomb is:
HE WAS KIND

[DORSINGTON]

The Weeds of Warwickshire

Their rotting bones lie scattered in each hedge;
I leant on one today and drank some beer,
Plucking at a rough leaf's double edge,
Conjuring the shade of what stood here

Before the beetle came, before the plague
Of death along each lane turned green to grey.
But memories are treacherous and vague,
Old photographs alone remain, today.

Armadas in full sail, fair emerald fleets,
The inshore squadron's glorious men-of-war,
Tall sentinels of shaded village streets,
Of warded pasture, hedge and cottage door.

'Elm Hateth man and Waiteth,' warn the crones,
'And all that walks upon two legs. Beware!
She'll Shed at nought to crush thy human bones;
Fey Fairy Queens Alone may shelter there.'

But elfin spell came never to their aid
As pestilence rained down in deadly tide,
And one by one those giants on parade
Succumbed to their peculiar suicide.

The Weeds of Warwickshire we called them once,
And shall again as centuries slide by —
These colonies of rotting stools and stumps
Will succour saplings blotting out the sky.

Man's span is short, his tribal lore truncate,
Yet *ulmus minor* flourishes below.
Within the dark her patient roots await
The passing of her parasitic foe.

[MUSTIQUE]

To human eyes, the onset of Dutch elm disease in Western Europe during the 1970's was a catastrophe. For elm trees, one suspects, it is a minor irritation, to be endured and overcome, just as it has been in the past and will be in the future. Elms are alive and well — flourishing even. It's just that we can't see them except as untidy shoots emerging from felled boles, 'testing the water', so to speak, for their parent roots and suckers which remain safe from the beetle in the sanctuary of the soil. And, yes, they did commit a form of suicide to combat this latest invasion, although arborealists will swiftly discount such notions as anthropomorphic nonsense. Well, perhaps. But it can't be denied that neither beetle or their pupae killed the elms. The Weeds of Warwickshire simply shut off their own sap and went underground, just as they have done in cycle after cycle for untold millennia.

In the Blood?

Nature or nurture or... Nietzsche?
Are we writ in the stars, or in clay?
Are the features of each of Gods creatures
Held ransom in random decay?

As Darwin sat scribbling his thesis
Of barnacles, beagles and men,
Was it predestination of species
Which guided the strokes of his pen?

Implacable as the creator,
The demons that urge us to mate;
Mother Nature's an iron dictator —
To multiply is to mutate.

It's wicked to think of, it's vicious,
But some kids are born little shits;
Before they can crawl they're malicious;
Rotten eggs sucking on tits.

Abandon the thought if you want, sir.
I leave it to parents to choose;
But I know of *one* little monster —
Please never ask me whose!

[DORSINGTON]

Specific Gravity

Though kith and kin may sacrifice their life,
   Though loyalty be bred into the bone,
Though God may bind together man and wife —
   Yet still the minds of men must quest alone.

Bequeath your children all the books you please,
   Or lead a horse to water in a drought —
The doors of revelation have their keys,
   Yet none may force the portal from without.

'Aye, nowt as strange as folk,' the Yorkies say,
   And said it since Neanderthal napped stone;
Though men join hands to ease each other's way —
   Yet still the mind of man quests on... alone.

[DORSINGTON]

How To Get Rich

Good fortune? The fact is
The more that you practise,
The harder you sweat,
The luckier you get.

Ideas? We've had 'em
Since Eve mated Adam,
But take it from me
Execution's the key.

The money? Just pester
A likely investor.
To get what you need
You toady to greed.

The talent? Go sign it!
But first, wine and dine it.
It's tedious work
With a talented jerk.

Good timing? To win it
You gotta be in it.
Just never be late
To quit or cut bait.

Expansion? It's vanity!
Profit is sanity.
Overhead begs
To walk on two legs.

The first step? Just do it
And bluff your way thru' it.
Remember to duck!
God speed...
and good luck!

[MUSTIQUE]

Space Craft

Nous appelons notre avenir l'ombre de lui-même que notre passé projette devant nous
What we call our future is the shadow which the past throws in front of us
— *Marcel Proust*

Like new loosed heifers, sleek and lean,
All winter held in barns close pinned,
We yearn for grass which none have seen,
Our small craft straws upon the wind —
Where no wind blows. And some, they say,
Have tombs which tumbled not to earth
But in the glare of endless day
Spin rudderless, the Void their berth,
Their solar wings and crippled sails
Computing readouts none can use,
While flocks of man-made nightingales
Sing out alerts to long-dead crews.

Yet whether from a weightless womb
Or from the vats of alchemy,
These words shall sound a planet's doom:
'*A child is born in Zero-G*'.

[CANDLEWOOD]

[87]

Life Support

*[With breathless thanks to the staff of
Danbury Hospital, Connecticut]*

Upon a bed of ice and fire,
  I waited, swathed in tube and wire,
    My lungs a searing funeral pyre;
      They asked me my religion — I was dying.
Prostrated in the fever's grip
  I watched an intravenous drip
    Pump ballast, then abandoned ship;
      'He's sinking!' cried a nurse. I thought: *I'm flying!*

Much later, while I convalesced
  I learned what I'd already guessed,
    When on his rounds, a quack confessed:
      'We nearly lost you, son. You just weren't trying.
I've seen it once or twice before,
  You wandered through an open door
    But can't remember what you saw...?'
      'You're right,' I said. And found that I was crying.

[MUSTIQUE]

'All the young dudes...'

All the young dudes, growin' old,
   Wanna get their story told,
Wanna see their names in print,
   Write a bio'— make a mint.

All the young dudes, wearin' specs,
   Waitin' on retirement cheques,
Takin' stairlifts up to heaven —
   Lift broke back in 'sixty-seven.

All the young dudes, gettin' frail,
   Hair a whiter shade of pale,
Thinkin' back to glory days,
   Memories a purple haze.

All the young dudes, short on cash,
   Hittin' wine insteada hash,
Got no use for LSD —
   Drugs come from the pharmacy.

All the young dudes — cut to fade,
   Gettin' limp insteada laid,
Life's a bitch and two's a crowd —
   Crank the volume way up loud.

[MUSTIQUE]

To those of us of a certain age, 1967 was...everything. Call it the summer of love. Call it the high point of sex 'n' drugs 'n' rock 'n' roll'. Call it any damn thing you want, but if you weren't there, especially in London or San Francisco...you wouldn't understand. Me? I was wandering up and down the Kings Road, Chelsea, with a snake-hipped, suede-booted blonde in white lipstick and spider web eyelashes, dressed myself in a full length military cloak and chiffon scarf, hair half way down my arse, imbibing green tea and hash in a hangout near World's End. Hey, for a 20 year old South London dude, it didn't get any cooler than that!

Mother Earth

Do not *trouble* yourselves on my account,
Nor put on airs, nor rave alone;
The teeth that snap,
The lips that flap,
The fist that shakes, I bred in the bone.
And your mother's heart is hard as stone.

Do not *trouble* yourselves with right or wrong,
For yours is not the only law;
The urge to blame,
The rage of shame
Has brought your house to peril's door.
And your mother forgave you, long before.

Do not *trouble* yourselves with shibboleths,
Nor seek to mend in blind despair;
The damage wrought
Is less than nought,
The price is more than a child could bear.
And your mother has long since ceased to care.

Envoi:

＊

I *forgive!*
(And you will forget — anon).
Look up!
The stars! *Now get you gone!*

Those who believe mankind capable of destroying the earth are, in my opinion, blinded by human self-importance. Certainly we are capable of making life on this planet uncomfortable, or impossible, for ourselves. But our influence pretty much stops there. Even if man were to loose every thermonuclear weapon he possessed, within a million or so years the planet would be crawling with diverse life forms. Within five or ten million years, it might prove difficult to detect any vestige of such a catastrophe. And, after all, five or ten million years is an eye blink in the measureless aeons the earth has supported life. As to the '*envoi*', it is what I suspect will happen, providing we give ourselves sufficient time to 'escape' from our mother planet — a thought which, on the face of it, is mad. Yet it represents but a complex extension of the migrations that have ruled the development of all species of life on the blue planet.

Intentions

What's an intention? A scarecrow of straw
Stuffed full of guilt in a field of
sighs.
My! How the crows of reality caw,
Perched on its heads, as they peck out its
eyes.

[MUSTIQUE]

Victory!

We fought for Peace and carried her, protesting
To battle, where we slaughtered, with much blood,
Her enemies. Their chieftains died contesting
Her remnant pieces, quartered in the mud.

[NEW YORK]

Waste

Nobody weeps for the dead;
We might as well weep at a wall.
We weep for ourselves instead;
We weep for the waste of it all.

When flesh has frittered its term
We lower the bone in the ground;
Why do we serve to the worm
What is kept from the faithful hound?

Nobody mourns for the dead;
We mourn what we cannot recall.
We mourn for the word unsaid;
We mourn for the waste of it all.

[MUSTIQUE]

My intention to have my remains mummified and interred in a purpose-built pyramid has been the subject of much (richly deserved) merriment among friends and in various newspapers. It is only an idle, slightly ridiculous whim. Were my remains to be chopped up and fed to my wonderful rare-breed Gloucester Old Spot or Middle White pigs, I can't say it would bother me much. The lines above were inspired by a news item concerning a man and his dog trapped in a cave by snow. The dog had consumed his master's corpse. My reaction to this was very far from the vehement horror evinced in the article.

Better Than Sex!

Though quacks claim physical exercise
    Will assist the spine to flex,
    And build to-die-for pecs,
    Or transform utter wrecks;
Still it's never, never, never, never,
    Never, never, ever, ever,
    Never ever better than sex!

                I've seen the surprise in a doxy's eyes
                When the filthy rich write cheques,
                Stuff caviar down their necks,
                Or buy them a gold Rolex;
                But it's never, never, never, never,
                Never, never, ever, ever,
                Never ever better than sex!

'Let's still be friends' is a tip to the wise
    That it's time to clear the decks,
    To collect all your effects,
    To pay your last respects
    And telephone up your ex';
It'll never, never, never, never,
    Never, never, ever, ever,
    Never be better than sex!

[MUSTIQUE]

[93]

Sign To Be Erected
At The Gate To Argyle Wood

It ate you up. I know it did.
They used you, then they turned away.
They used Your Honour, then they hid
Their pretty little toys away.

They laughed at you. I heard them laugh.
Wrong tie; wrong club; wrong bloody school.
They never saw the better half.
I did. Now rest, you daft old fool.

Here's glory from your enemy
That never was, sir. God forbid.
They tricked you, but they shan't trick me.
It ate you up. I know it did.

[MUSTIQUE]

Michael Argyle was the judge at the OZ Trial held in Court Number 2 at The Old Bailey in the summer of 1971. Despite his highly partial summing up, the jury found my co-defendants and me not guilty of the only serious charge of which we were accused — 'Conspiracy to Pervert the Morals of the Young of the Realm'. Despite this, Argyle sentenced us to prison in what even *The Times* described as 'an act of establishment revenge'. That he had cocked up the longest 'obscenity' trial in British history (from the Establishment's point of view) was made abundantly clear by Lord Chief Justice Widgery's comments at the Court of Appeal some months later. Yet Argyle's treatment from the powers that be following this debacle was almost as shabby and dubious as the trial itself. They simply ignored and demoted him. Argyle was a victim, not a perpetrator. The simple truth is that he was selected as the OZ Trial judge because he was expendable. He will have a wood named after him within the forest of his 'enemy that never was', not in mockery, but as a memento from one victim to another. A bad judge, but not a bad man.

Shields

Warrior, know your shield a two-edged weight,
Constricting as it blocks the killing blow.
The drawn bridge bars escape by Western gate,

While ramparts hide besiegers far below;
Thus sanctuary is turned to blazing trap,
And iron armour freezes in the snow.

All shields exact the price of handicap,
No turtle ever raced the wind-borne hare,
Nor porcupine e'er nestled in a lap.

No woman ever held me in her snare
To pierce my heart with tenderness as bait,
To bring me squalling brats to call my heir.

I stand before you now, inviolate.
Warrior! Know your shield a two-edged weight!

[DORSINGTON]

Amazing Grace

[for Rear Admiral Grace Murray Hopper]

A counter-clockwise clock:
 Tock-tick, tock-tick, tick-tock.
  The budget's chock-a-block,
   The project's in dry dock.

Abandon ship? Who'll tell her
 She's fouled her own propeller?
  You'll need ear-plugs young fellah —
   She's a salty Cinderella!

Amazing Grace won't buy it,
 (It's not that she'll *defy* it):
  "If questioned, just deny it,
   But, whatever happens — *try it!*"

[MUSTIQUE]

Strange that one of the most inspirational people I have ever read about should be a Rear Admiral in the US Navy. Grace Murray Hopper was the co-inventor of COBOL, an important early computer programming language which made it possible to instruct computers using words rather than numbers. Her survival and rise in the male dominated world of the US armed forces speaks volumes for her abilities and guts. Hopper was a legend in the American Navy when she retired 'involuntarily' aged eighty, after 43 years of service. She was often credited with launching or supporting what appeared to her superiors to be 'hare-brained schemes' — only to be vindicated later. These ideas included using computers to track the life cycle of crop eating locusts, building a weather computer and tracking the waves at the bottom of the ocean. She smoked unfiltered Lucky Strike cigarettes and kept a clock in her office that ran counter-clockwise, to remind herself time was 'running out' rather than 'going by'. There are many versions of the famous sign on her desk. I chose years ago to make one of them the official motto of my publishing company: "If it's a good idea, go ahead and do it. It's much easier to apologise than it is to get permission." She died in 1992 aged 85.

'Shadow Billy'

"By God, I wish that I
Were twenty-five year younger.
I'd blacken up yer eye!
There's not a man among yer!"

The bouncers put him right
And sent him down the 'Dilly:
"He does it every night —
They call him 'Shadow Billy'.

"He wouldn't hurt a fly,"
They grinned in recollection —
"That is, unless his eye
Detects his own reflection!"

[MUSTIQUE]

'Shadow Billy' was a Soho character in the middle 80's, well known to bouncers, coppers and door-men alike. He only ever attacked his own reflection. The 'Dilly is Piccadilly Circus, of course.

Trouble

Out of the mail, your mouth still yawning,
Out of the phone by your bed at night,
Out of the blue on a glorious morning,
Suddenly, everything's not alright.
Trouble. Trouble.
Suddenly, everything's not alright.

Out of the mouth of a friendly stranger,
Out of the crease of a lover's frown,
Out of the cry of a child in danger,
Suddenly, everything's upside-down.
Trouble. Trouble.
Suddenly, everything's upside-down.

Out of a rain of boots and curses,
Out of the barrel of some fool's gun,
Out of the eyes of hospital nurses,
Suddenly, everything's come undone.
Trouble. Trouble.
Everything under the sun — undone.

[MUSTIQUE]

An Old Dog Is The Best Dog

An old dog is the best dog,
A dog with rheumy eyes;
An old dog is the best dog
A dog grown sad and wise,
    Not one who snaps at bubbles,
        Nor one who barks at nowt,
            A dog who knows your troubles,
            A dog to see you out.

An old bitch is the best bitch,
Not pups to fetch your sticks;
An old bitch is the best bitch,
Not one to teach new tricks,
    Not one who's up and leaping,
        But one whose coat is grey,
            Leg's twitching while she's sleeping
            In dreams of yesterday.

[MUSTIQUE]

The Proof
[For Dick Pountain]

Knowledge comes but hard and slow,
   And much is hid that once we knew.
Much there is we cannot know;
   Or, if we know, we misconstrue.

Gods are built on faith and prayer,
   And faith demands divinity;
Math alone is truth laid bare,
   The proof of all infinity.

Prime is prime, no ifs or buts,
   Immutable as '3', '1', '7';
You do not 'feel it in your guts':
   Prime on earth *is* prime in heaven.

[MUSTIQUE]

In his amusing biography of Paul Erdös *The Man Who Loved Only Numbers*, Paul Hoffman quotes the number theorist G. H. Hardy on the beauty and rigour of numbers which he believed 'constitute the true fabric of the universe.' Hardy postulated that the mathematician 'is in much more direct contact with reality [than a physicist] who deals with the subject matter usually described as 'real'. 317 is a prime, not because we think it is so, or because our minds are shaped in one way rather than another, but because it is so, because mathematical reality is built that way.'

Spot The Difference

One marvels at
    the infinite variety of souls
        who crew this ship of fools,
            adrift upon an endless sea —

Sans chart or map,
    the rotting superstructure shot with holes,
        while with their toy-town tools
            men launch the lifeboats endlessly.

Or is it that
    the superstructure rots within our souls
        while endless drifts of fools
            of infinite variety —

Their maps aflap,
    in shot-up ships, chart out on lifeboat shoals,
        sans crew, their toy-town rules
            to launch into eternity?

[MUSTIQUE]

'When mercy strains your patience...'
[For Steve and Lynn Caldwell]

When mercy strains your patience, son,
    When strangers ask for more,
When common sense says you have done
    Enough — throw wide your door!

'The world is too much with us' said
    The poet — he was wise:*
Why miss the chance of breaking bread
    With angels in disguise?

[MUSTIQUE]

*'The world is too much with us; late and soon,
  Getting and spending, we lay waste our powers:'
— William Wordsworth

'Knowing isn't doing...'

Knowing isn't doing if there's nothing to be done;
Doing minus knowing's only bluffing on the run;
    Knowing isn't doing;
    Doing isn't knowing;
Nothing but the knowing plus the doing gets it done.

[HIGHFIELD]

[103]

The Wedding Dress

The woodland trees are decked in reds,
The scarlet blush of newly-weds
Impatient on their wedding night —
Fresh-minted gold their shy delight.

Now jilted summer stands aside
As autumn claims his burning bride,
Arrayed in all her finery,
Displayed for all the world to see.

But honeymoons are short, if sweet,
And time flies by on raptured feet;
Too soon a tyrant's icy stare
Will fall upon fair limbs laid bare.

So I will walk in autumn mist
To see the bride before she's kissed,
Collecting up her leaves to press
A memory — her wedding dress.

[DORSINGTON]

The Troubles

As I was passing Dublin Gate,
I met a man who dined on hate,
    Who supped upon a sea of song
Made bitter by an ancient wrong.

As I passed through a Belfast mist,
I met a man who shook his fist,
    Who preyed upon the men of hate
Who crept at night through Dublin Gate.

As I was passing Cromwell Street,
I met a man blown off his feet,
    Who scrawled in blood upon a stone:
No prisoners! God will know His own!

As I was passing Parliament,
I met a man whose orders sent
    Young squaddies out upon the street
To shoot at men they'd never meet.

As I was passing New York State,
I met a man who heaped a plate
    With others' pain; who paid a fee
To be a part of history.

As I passed by a widow's door
I heard a cry: *Dear Christ, no more!*
    A pox upon your Dublin Gate,
You Belfast mist... your men of hate.

[NEW YORK]

Dead White Males

They tell me that postmodernism's in the saddle now,
Having swapped its thoroughbred to mount a sacred cow;
Laying waste the landscape of a culture as it rails
In righteous deconstruction of...
    Dead White Males.

They tell me indiscriminate discrimination rules;
Eurocentric rubbish has been scoured from our schools;
There's no room in curriculums for sexist fairy tales
To sow the seeds of tyrannies from...
    Dead White Males.

They tell me multicultural academies must rid
Their blushing shelves of Shakespeare — or Chaucer, God forbid!
For Raleigh, Swift and Dickens and Wordsworth in his dales,
Walt Whitman, Donne and Tennyson are...
    Dead White Males.

Envoi
    "D.W.M.s,
Chuck 'em in the Thames.
Plait a rope and string a gallows,
To the libraries! Wheelbarrows!
Strip the stacks of books by liars —
Shred 'em! Hurl 'em in the fires!
That'll learn 'em, those who wrote 'em,
Saw their balls off at the scrotum!
Fetch a hammer! Fetch the nails!
Crucify all
Dead White Males!"

[CANDLEWOOD]

"A minefield of unimaginable minorities waiting to be offended" — Harold Evans on American Universities. Political Correctness of any stripe starts with the best of intentions — as a clarion call. It then passes through various stages — as an irritating background whine or strident name-calling, for instance — until, at last, it emerges as the massed braying of lunatic donkeys. Unfortunately, all that is needed for the adherents of this New Ignorance to wield real power is for people to do nothing. In an age of information technology, sticks and stones <u>can</u> break your bones!

The Serpent's Gift

I dissemble,
You dissemble,
We dissemble,
Lying straight, or slantly by omission;
    So, will the Prince of Liars
    Cast us all into the fires
As punishment? Or are we competition?

See no evil?
Speak no evil?
Hear no evil?
'Lord, not yet!' Augustine's hollow vow.
    The Magi in their trammels
    Dreamt of sherbet, not of camels;
Holy hermits know the 'why' but not the 'how'.

'Little liar!'
'Pants on fire!'
'Porky-pie-er!'
When creeps deceit into a child's mind;
    And are their fibs acquired,
    Or do they come hard-wired?
Are the mouths of babes the sum of humankind?

I dissemble,
You dissemble,
We dissemble;
A veil of lies to cloak a vale of tears;
    A camouflage of kindness,
    The serpent's gift of blindness;
The cataracts that soften wasted years.

[CANDLEWOOD]

[108]

A Poet's Consolation

Beside broad streams of hieroglyphic flood
   The battlements of prose are raised in vain;
Their clay decays, subsiding into mud —
   While diamond shards of verse alone remain.

[SOHO]

'I had a friend...'

I had a friend whom once I thought I knew,
Yet no man knows another's heart, entire;
He killed himself and damn near killed me, too —
The dead are no less dead by friendly fire.

[MUSTIQUE]

'The House that Crack Built...'

This is the house that crack built.

This is the pipe
That lay in the house that crack built.

This is the puff,
That filled the pipe
That lay in the house that crack built.

This is the stuff,
That would not puff,
That filled the pipe
That lay in the house that crack built.

This is the sod,
That sold the stuff,
That would not puff,
That filled the pipe
That lay in the house that crack built.

This is the gun with the barrel sawn,
That shot the sod,
That sold the stuff,
That would not puff,
That filled the pipe
That lay in the house that crack built.

This is the room with the curtains drawn
That hid the gun with the barrel sawn,
That shot the sod,
That sold the stuff,
That would not puff,
That filled the pipe
That lay in the house that crack built.

This is the man who slept at dawn,
That lived in the room with the curtains drawn,
That sold the gun with the barrel sawn,
That shot the sod,
That sold the stuff,
That would not puff,
That filled the pipe
That lay in the house that crack built.

This is the frock all tattered and torn,
That kept the man who slept at dawn,
That lived in the room with the curtains drawn,
That sold the gun with the barrel sawn,
That shot the sod,
That sold the stuff,
That would not puff,
That filled the pipe
That lay in the house that crack built.

This is the maiden all forlorn,
That wore the frock all tattered and torn,
That kept the man who slept at dawn,
That lived in the room with the curtains drawn,
That sold the gun with the barrel sawn,
That shot the sod,
That sold the stuff,
That would not puff,
That filled the pipe
That lay in the house that crack built.

This is the babe that never was born,
That died in the womb of a maid forlorn,
That wore the frock all tattered and torn,
That kept the man who slept at dawn,
That lived in the room with the curtains drawn,
That sold the gun with the barrel sawn,
That shot the sod,
That sold the stuff,
That would not puff,
That filled the pipe
That lay in the house that crack built.

[MUSTIQUE]

I know only too well of what I speak in this poem. My advice to anyone about to try crack is as follows: Firstly, it will cost you more than you can pay. Secondly, it will play havoc with your health in a very short time. Thirdly, because your personality will change, most of your friends will disown you — just as you will lose interest in anyone not taking or selling crack. Fourthly, you will almost certainly become addicted (and super-paranoid) very quickly indeed. Lastly, unless you quit early (difficult) and permanently (very, very difficult) the lifestyle and the drug itself will conspire to kill you. Apart from all that, it's great!

A Discovery in Wandsworth

Whilst turnin' aht me attic
A faded photograph
Flutters to the floorboards.
I 'ears me nephew laugh:

"An' who the devil's this, then,
I niver would have guessed!
That's you, nah, uncle ain't it?
But whoo's this, 'alf-undressed?"

I stuff it in me pocket,
(How strong old passions grip!)
Me loins and ticker surgin',
A finger to me lip.

Our eyes creep to the kitchen
Two floors beneaf: "It's wise
To hask a man no questions,
To save from 'earin' lies."

He shrugs a bony shoulder
As we go dahn for tea.
He's starin' 'ard at aunty,
But niver looks at me!

[DORSINGTON]

Gulliver Sneesby

Gulliver Sneesby, child of shame,
    Deplored that he was born a fella,
He tried and tried to change his name
    To Isabella.

Gulliver played the bore at large,
    A feminist in tyrant's clothing;
He wore his zeal to camouflage
    His own self-loathing.

Gulliver wrestled, wracked with guilt,
    Tormented by debased desires;
He fantasized himself rebuilt,
    With surgeon's pliers.

Gulliver scoured the dictionary
    While etymologists debated,
He wanted half the OED
    To be castrated.

Gulliver sneered at marriage vows,
    As 'sexist tricks to chain and fetter',
He sighed for those pathetic cows
    Who knew no better.

Gulliver Sneesby, mother's son,
    A prophet who gained little credit;
He wrote a tome which weighed a ton,
    But no-one read it.

[CANDLEWOOD]

Apologies to Edward Arlington Robinson and his masterpiece, Miniver Cheevy. Whenever I am down, I only have to think of the lines: "He missed the medieval grace / Of iron clothing" to put me to rights. I must apologise, too, to Guy Sneesby, the internet genius at Dennis Interactive in London. Guy is absolutely nothing like the wretch described above, but I simply could not resist using his family name. (Note: OED: The Oxford English Dictionary. The 'definitive historical dictionary of the English language')

Why Do They Do It?

["I could never be a politician. I couldn't bear to
be right all the time." — Sir Peter Ustinov]

Why do they do it? Why do they do it?
Why do they stand on their hind legs lying —
Lying and lying and lying and lying —
Even though everyone knows that they do it?
Even though everyone mutters: I knew it!
I knew it, I knew it! I <u>knew</u> they were lying!
Lying when even their mothers aren't buying.
How can they do it?   *How* can they do it?
Spinning a web til they're lost in the thick of it,
Topping the knob til we're all of us sick of it,
Sick of the pack of 'em, spouters and stammerers,
Whining in microphones, preening for cameras,
Bullying, blaming and always denying —
And lying and lying and lying and *lying.*

[DORSINGTON]

[115]

A Lullaby for Bottles

Here we lie in stony quiet,
Far below the lamplit halls,
Troubled not by human riot,
Safe within our weeping walls.

Sleep my brethren, dream and sleep,
Row on row and line by line;
May your dreams be dark and deep,
You who guard the living wine.

Here is comfort, here is nectar.
Here is comradeship compressed.
Here lie we, the vine's protector,
While the fruit of ages rest.

Sleep my brethren, dream and sleep,
Row on row and line by line;
You have promises to keep,
You who guard the living wine.

[SOHO]

[116]

'Oh, do not call them vultures...'

Oh, do not call them vultures, for vultures love dead meat
And rarely don disguises or lurk across the street.
Not so your tabloid journalist who craves his victims fresh,
To feed the willing multitudes who lust for living flesh.

Oh, do not call them jackals, such epithets are crude,
A journo slays for shillings, a jackal hunts for food.
No more are they hyenas; hyenas do not laugh
While nosing through their vomit for one last paragraph.

Oh, do not call them leeches, they've heard all that before,
And leeches have their uses — they gorge upon a war;
They worship trains derailing, they feast on plague or flood:
Yet were we to ignore them, they'd fade for lack of blood!

[DORSINGTON]

Scapegoats

Men smile at superstitions, fingers crossed —
    Barabbas rapped on wood — they let him go.
Yet Pontius Pilate diced with Christ and lost —
    All scapegoats have their uses — cross or no.

[MUSTIQUE]

[118]

Prodigal Son

Often I ventured in Babylon's towers,
    Never a friend I met — never a one,
    Playing the part of the prodigal son.
Many the weeks and many the hours,
Barely a moment to think of the flowers
    Patiently budding in Warwickshire's air.
    Never a thought of a snapdragon there,
Or May on the hedge. All of my powers
    Spent upon gilding the lilies of gain,
While blue-eyed forget-me-nots lowered their gaze,
    Their beauty unmourned in an English lane.
Yet now, as I lie amidst Babylon's maze,
    Decked in the trappings of fabulous dross,
    By the sirens of night, I weep for their loss.

[NEW YORK]

[119]

The Fool

My friend would ask me, curious,
  When we were lads in school,
'You know it makes 'em furious,
  Why play the bloody fool?'

My mother she would scold me
  Or lecture me in tears;
How many times she told me
  To emulate my peers.

When I was one and twenty,
  My editor would say:
'You've talent here aplenty,
  Why play the fool all day?'

And even my true lover
  In gentleness will ask,
'I love you like no other,
  Think you I love the mask?'

Their faces set like thunder,
  The men with gravitas,
The men whose gold I plunder
  Each time I play the ass —

Too late they learn their danger
  In breach of fortune's rule,
That Lady Luck's a stranger
  To pride, but loves a fool.

[SOHO]

Chinese Whispers

[On looking into a dozen anthologised versions of
'On First Looking Into Chapman's Homer' by John Keats]

A comma here, a comma there,
Apostrophes inserted;
The stanza split to make a fit,
Indented lines inverted.

A semicolon gone astray,
And here, its tail deleted;
A second 'n' in Darien,
The error then repeated.

Ah, publishers are hasty men
Who like their bread with honey;
To proof a rhyme demands one's time,
And time, dear sir, is money!

[DORSINGTON]

[121]

Knowing When To Go

Some go early — lucky them,
The eulogies are frightful;
Some expire, *cherchez la femme,*
With relatives grown spiteful.
Some go gently, two by two,
Simpatico forever,
Some cling on, like me and you,
Through any kind of weather.
Some go screaming in the dark
With demons dancing madly,
Some go witty, some go stark,
The damaged goods go gladly.
Some go sudden, swept away
Fiddling, fey, like Neros,
Some defiant, stags at bay,
The way of unsung heroes.
Some, like cats, creep out alone
To join their feral brothers.
Some are gone before they're grown
To break the hearts of mothers.
Some go vicious, some go wise,
The saddest like a robot,
The best with starlight in their eyes —
Though where they go, I know not.

[MUSTIQUE]

Cause and Effect

['...*what is found in the effect is already in the cause.*'
— Henri Bergson L'Évolution Criétrice]

A wayward pebble clatters down the scree:
A minute later roars the avalanche.
A beetle buries eggs within a branch:
A decade passes; falls the stricken tree.
A microscopic virus in the breath:
A deadly battle waged within the veins.
A fungal spore mutates and famine reigns.
A word misspoke and comes a lover's death.
A poet makes a pass at someone's wife:
A fumbled gene aborted in the dawn.
A moment's hesitation with the knife:
A limbless Michelangelo is born.
A billion years without a sign of life:
A whisper from the gods— amoeba spawn.

[MUSTIQUE]

Marchesa Casati's Party

Marchesa Casati is holding a party,
It's terribly arty with Nubian slaves
And boa constrictors as luminous fixtures,
Draped upon pictures of virgins in caves.

The cost is colossal, her husband's a fossil,
A recent apostle of avant-garde art;
Though supra-exotic and faintly erotic
I hear she's neurotic and given to fart.

Her crows are albino, imported from Reno,
The leopard's called Fino, he's terribly brave
And once ate a flunky dressed up as a monkey...
Or was it a junkie who wouldn't behave?

Her jewels are Nirvana, she rides Lippizaner
And slips live piranha in gentlemen's beer,
She's sadomachismo and fondles a gizmo,
God knows what it is, though I have an idea.

Her set is precocious, her pets are ferocious,
Her guests are atrocious and some of them low;
Marchesa Casati is holding a party,
It's terribly arty — I think I shall go!

[DORSINGTON]

Marchesa Luisa Casati thrived in Rome in the early 1900's. Her hair was dyed orange framing a ghostly face adorned with mascara terminating in two-inch long eyelashes. She was a recluse for much of her life but gave fabulous parties which shamed and enraged her rivals. Her hobbies included encouraging avant-garde artists and keeping a menagerie of exotic and often dangerous pets. Spending more than one fortune without apparent restraint, she ended up penniless in London where, according to Lord Berner's biographer, Marc Amory, 'she showed uncomplaining courage.' I have embellished a little in my verse (I do not know anything about her husband(s)) but not by much, I suspect. Modern day goths and punks — on you knees!

Sex With Your Ex

Less guilt,
Less wilt,

Less nag;
More shag.

[NEW YORK]

From the headline brain-storming session for the December 2001 edition of *Stuff* magazine, edited by Greg Gutfeld In NYC.

The World's Last Choir

And so they came, the living and the dead;
Quiet, unconcerned with their condition
Or their status, by love of music led,
Each lover of his separate volition,
The rope of lies too short to warp their way.
They sung at no command, their throats combined,
A mighty host whose dust would dark the day
Were such dust present; the sighted and the blind,
The halt, the lame and those whose flesh had long
Since passed into the mystery of song.
In fugal thrall, bound up by chords of praise
They sung the waning law of earthly days
In unison, their voices ever higher
On that last day, and they — the world's last choir.

[NEW YORK]

Fast Awake

When I was young I fell asleep
   And dreamt I sailed upon a sea
Where dreams were real enough, and cheap.
   We called the sea: *Reality.*

The colours of the world have leached,
   My skin is creased, my fingers shake;
I woke to find the barky beached.
   Spiced foods give me the belly-ache.

I wonder if I'm fast awake
   Or dreaming still? I wouldn't know.
The sea is shrunk into a lake —
   And where did all the mermaids go?

[SOHO]

'Mighty the ant to an aphid...'

Mighty the ant to an aphid,
   Mighty the spider to fly,
Mighty the tiger to bullock,
   Mighty the mink to a nye;

Mighty the urchin to beetle,
   Mighty the fox to a foal,
Mighty the cuckoo to robin,
   Mighty the hawk to a vole.

Mighty the weasel to coney,
   Mighty the wolf to a dog,
Mighty the lion to jackal,
   Mighty the jackal to hog;

Mighty the bailiff to peasant,
   Mighty the power of the pen,
Yet, mightier, love,
     than all the above
  Is the tongue of a woman
    — to men!

[35,000 FEET MID ATLANTIC]

'If death knows no dominion...'

If death knows no dominion,
  The dead wield iron claws:
Ghost limbs aligned to pinion,
  To bend us to their cause.

By hoary yews and birches
  We worship gods they chose;
We sweep their empty churches,
  We smite their ancient foes.

If death knows no dimension,
  The dead are with us still;
By custom — and convention,
  They wed us to their will.

Their art a thing of beauty,
  The bait by which we're led;
Little we bring but duty
  To serve the ghastly dead.

[NEW YORK]

Written after reading 'And Death Shall Have No Dominion' by Dylan Thomas one fine fall night having just viewed the surreal wreckage of The World Trade Center under arc lights. Surreal or not, I was shaken to the core at the horrifying evidence of how history binds us all in the chains of old hatreds and mutual loathing. Dylan Thomase died a few blocks from where I wrote the above lines.

Surreal Deal

[And the Devil whoops as he whooped of old:
'It's clever, but is it Art?' — Rudyard Kipling]

I fixed the lion-bicycle
And fed the furry cup;
I polished Marcel's urinal,
(Some Mutt had blocked it up).

I used the lobster telephone
To call my Dada's brute,
But Salvador was not at home
And Isidore was mute.

Magritte told me a secret when
I mentioned André's twins:
He told me they had eaten them
To wash away their sins.

I don't believe those babies died,
I've heard they're still around,
Installing bricks for Maldehyde —
And charging by the pound!

[DORSINGTON]

Aleister

['Do what thou wilt shall be the whole of the Law.'
— A. Crowley The Book of the Law (1909)]

Aleister did what he wilt,
But it wasn't the whole of the law;
(Once you eradicate guilt
Banality takes to the floor).

Charlatans loathe what they build,
They leave their disciples to rot;
Aleister did what he willed,
But smashed all the toys in his cot.

Aleister's calling on Thoth,
While pentagrams hiss on the floor;
He's raising the demons of wrath —
But nobody cares anymore.

[DORSINGTON]

Crowley was a diabolist and self-styled magician during the late 19th century magical revival in Britain. He liked to be described as 'The Great Beast' or 'The Wickedest Man Alive' and went by the numerical pseudonym '666'. Utterly besotted with his own notoriety, he filled newspapers of the time with stories of drugs, orgies and sacrificial rites. A prolific but feeble poet, he was a member of The Order of the Golden Dawn along with W B Yeats, but left after a row about his cabalistic status. Think of him as a slightly less vicious, better educated and bald version of Charlie Manson and you won't be far wrong.

A Norman Priest Dreams of the English

How now, this cross-grained mongrel breed
Of foul-mouthed curs — thieves all! — their tongue
A sticky coil of stolen dung,
Who, ceaseless, on their betters feed;
And like some choking, noxious weed
Run riot where once roses sprung,
Their hybrid coarseness careless flung
On silk hard won by word and deed.
They nothing know but where to strike
Their enemies, these pearl-struck swine
Who piss in fountains, foul oaths hurled
At slattern wench or priest alike.
And yet! I dreamt a dream. a sign!
These oafs — Sweet Christ! — will rule the world!

[DORSINGTON]

The Shield of Art

All art deceives — the mind if not the eye;
A finger pointing at the moon, confused
With lunar beauty. Thus is nature used
To cross the 't' in Art and dot the 'i'
In Hubris. Spelt with a capital 'A',
'tongue-tied by Authority', suspended
To impress, (and, yes, the pun intended).
Yet art is not a thing. It is the way
By which men may reveal themselves as gods,
Arresting time. Made mad with loveliness,
The commonplace sublime, our craft sure signs
That though the Truth lays on with bloody rods
Men may endure; and as they groan, confess
Their Art is but a shield — as are these lines!

[52,000 FEET]

*Suggested by Nietzsche: 'We have Art in that we may not perish
from the Truth'. The phrase 'tongue-tied by Authority' comes from
Shakespeare, Sonnet lxvi*

'What time is it?'

The sands of time
    Race through the glass
As gravity requires,
    Each grain a mime
      Of dusty farce,
A silent rain of liars.

The child at play,
    The man condemned,
New lovers at their pleasure;
    To such the sway
      Of time is hemmed
In grudging miser's measure.

The child at school,
    The lover spurned,
The galley slave who cowers;
    Watch now the rule
      Of time upturned
As minutes pass like hours.

'What time is it?'
    Who knows? Not I,
As Father Time — that traitor!
    The stars have writ
      His true reply:
'Much later — always later.'

[MUSTIQUE]

[133]

On Reading Dead Rhymers

I read the Hound of Heaven aloud
  and sought to catch my breath;
    Here Dead Lie We ashamed my craven heart.
Proud Raleigh's Even Such is Time
  swapped blasphemies with death.
    Wise Landor stood, full ready to depart.

In fright I fled from That Good Night,
  a wailing mere to sail;
    then crawled, appalled to cross the moaning bar;
Near spent, I entered Shelley's peace
  by way of Reading Gaol —
    at Charlotte's muse, I crossed a bridge too far.

*

'Enough, enough!' my lover cried;
  'Cease now and come to bed.'
    I marked my place but cannot face
  the lines I have not read —
  the unQuick on the Dead.

[DORSINGTON]

Here Be Dragons

We've mapped the mountains of the moon,
   The lava fields of mars,
We map the trails of migrant whales,
   We map the farthest stars.

We map the ocean's shifting shore,
   We've mapped the open sky,
The treasure rooms of Inca tombs
   And where the ley lines lie.

We map the spots upon the sun,
   We map the human gene;
The medics' knives took endless lives
   To map the soft machine.

We'd map the seven plains of hell
   If Satan gave the sign,
(All tyrants feed upon the need
   To move a dotted line).

We've mapped the bloody universe
   And pinned it in a net,
But as for charts of human hearts —
   We've made no progress yet!

[DORSINGTON]

The Protestors

The Opposition Debates
A Government Sponsored
Parliamentary Pay Rise

We protest! We
Know best. We

Are right. We
Shall fight. We

Demure. We
Are sure. We

Shall win. We
Give in.

[CANDLEWOOD]

With apologies and in gratitude to Gwendolyn Brooks. Her marvelous poem 'We Real Cool' published in 1960 was instrumental in my conversion to poetry back when my hair was half way down to my snakeskin boots!

The Box

Within a room to which none but myself
              May hold the key,
       High up upon a dusty shelf
       And even there, kept privately,
There sits a locked and battered box of tin,
              With nothing in.

With nothing in, at least, of any worth
              To man or beast
        In heaven or this hell on earth —
       Excepting only 'the deceased';
A trifle bootless heirs might chance to find,
             And pay no mind.

The box is lined in cedar, stained in red —
           I know not why.
        Some careless owner, long since dead,
        Has sketched within the lid an eye,
Long-lashed, slant-lidded, sly, with malice there.
            I know that stare.

Yet few would care to keep a battered box
            Of any kind,
        And chances are that once the locks
        Are broken it will be consigned
To rank oblivion. And there will stay,
           Til Judgment Day.

Yet who can say, when truth is held in thrall
          To save one soul?
       For I have not the wherewithal
        Or strength to give back what I stole —
If such might be within my gift or lot.
          Which it is not.

[MUSTIQUE]

To A Beautiful Lady
of a Certain Age

Lady, lady do not weep —
What is gone is gone. Now sleep.
Turn your pillow, dry your tears,
Count thy sheep and not thy years.

Nothing good can come of this.
Time rules all, my dearest, 'tis
But folly to be waging war
On one who never lost before.

Lady, this is all in vain,
Youth can never come again;
We have drunk the summer wine,
None can make a stitch in time.

Nip and tuck 'til crack of doom,
What is foretold in the womb
May not be forsworn with gold —
Nor may time be bought or sold.

Dearest, do I love thee less,
Do I shrink from thy caress?
Think you I could cease to care?
Never was there one so fair!

Lady, lady do not weep —
What is gone is gone. Now sleep.
Lean against me, calm your fears,
Count thy blessings, not thy years.

[MUSTIQUE]

If all commercially minded cosmetic surgeons were tied end to end along a railway track — that
would be me stoking the train without a qualm in the world.

Soho Sestina

Champagne and neon bubbles frame the doors
Of yet another strip joint. Up the street,
Two constables are eyeing up the whores
Leant cross-legged by the walls to spare their feet.
It's early yet. A cat with bandaged paws
Is rooting in a bin to fish out meat.

Three sailors, on the scrounge for fresher meat,
Inspect the winking sign above the doors;
They stand there as the neon bubbly pours
An endless stream of blessings on the street.
The girls roll up their eyes in mock defeat —
They've got a sense of humour, Soho whores:

They know the joke about 'the sailor's 'ores
And tiller girls'. Plenty of time to meet
More likely joes. A scrape of coppers' feet
And they're away, through alleyways and doors,
Gazelles in flight, up stairs and down the street.
The coppers swagger by without a pause.

The cat surveys the sailors through its paws
Poised on its bin, as one by one the whores'
Stilettos echo down the cobbled street.
The sailors shrug and step inside to meet
A hostess, who will tell them she adores
It, even as she pours it (dexterous feat!)

Into a pot secreted by her feet.
Her topless friends will titter while she pours
Them bottle after bottle. Back outdoors,
A junkie pimp is beating on his whores
And threatening them both that he will mete
Out worse: Now get your arses on the street!

A prossie walks a john to some back street;
Slips out a condom, kneels down by his feet,
Unzips his fly and slips it on his meat...
Then squeals! An alley cat with bandaged paws
Has brushed her leg! She flees. From fire doors
A bouncer throws three sailors to the whores —

Some early meat. A pause for blistered feet
From scores of tired whores in darkened doors;
But then, it's always early — on the street.

[MUSTIQUE]

I first came across a sestina propped up in bed, appropriately enough, in my Soho flat some years ago. I was recovering from serious over indulgence and something about the odd repetition of the lines helped to turn my attention from a pounding hangover. This was the first time I ever made marginal notes in pencil in a book of poetry (*Other Men's Flowers*) as I painstakingly figured out the ABCDEF, FAEBDC, CFBADE continuum in Rudyard Kipling's 'Sestina Of The Tramp-Royal.' Said to have been invented in Provence in the 13th century by the French troubadour poet, Arnaut Daniel, sestinas have also been known as the 'songs of sixes'. Poets as diverse as Swinburne, Auden, Sir Philip Sydney and Elizabeth Bishop have turned their skilful hands to this tricky, intoxicating form. For my first attempt, which came out in a marathon all-nighter rush, I found myself compounding the difficulty by rhyme. It was huge fun!

Ed

[Tombstone for Ed Barker]

Ed, you silly bugger!
Damn your woolly hide,
What d'yer think yer playin' at?
Annie, stand aside!
Rouse yourself now Eddie!
Draw me something, son!

Barker! Are you listenin'?
Annie! Christ, he's gone!
Run away and left us,
Kiboshed! Bought the farm!
Ed, you had it all, lad,
Ripcord looks and charm,

Razor wit and talent.
I can't believe you're dead.
Pardon me for asking...

...Why'd you do it,
Ed?

[MUSTIQUE]

The death of any friend is painful. That of Edward Barker, a soft-eyed, quick-witted, one-off-the-wrist cartoonist of immense likability and charm still bewilders and angers me in equal measure. Ed drank himself to death. But why? We bought Ed his 'last supper' consisting of every forbidden food known to man (I recall *foie gras*, olives, salami, oysters and lager) at his hospital bed. His doctors told us it didn't matter anymore what he ate or drank. I ranted at him for a minute or two as described above (Annie is a *nom de guerre*, by the way) but received only a knowing wink and a smart-arse reply for my pains. He died not long afterwards. Why, Ed? Why?

Warm Round a Fiver

There's some of 'em warm round a fiver,
An' tight as a clam round a score,
And some as can't 'elp 'emselves, neiver —
But what are they *saving* it for?

There's some of 'em trainin' as misers,
An' some as don' care what yer think,
But whether they're plungers or risers,
The devil they'll buy yer a drink!

There's some as makes feeble excuses
In pubs, as they heads for the door,
An' some as don' know what abuse is,
But what are they *saving* it for?

There's some as admit being thrifty,
An' some as keep changin' their wills,
But ask 'em for change for a fifty
An' watch 'em grow green at the gills!

There's some of 'em blusters an' chortles,
There's some of 'em wired at the jaw,
But I notice that none are immortals:
So *what are they saving it for?*

[MUSTIQUE]

*I am indebted to Sharon Islam for the wonderful expression
'warm round a fiver', which I believe I originally heard used to
describe my old friend, Don Atyeo — totally unjustifiably, of course!*

Dead Gods

'Thou shalt have no other gods before me.'
(You note the plural usage — lower case?)
Thus the God of Hebrews, wreathed in glory,
Set wrath in stone to chide his chosen race.

'Twas ever thus, in manuscript or mural,
The gods command and trembling men obey.
Yet often I have pondered on that plural:
The deathless gods — the gods of yesterday.

Who prays to feathered serpent, Quetzalcoatl?
Who to one-eyed Woden, lord of war?
Who praises Bacchus, god of flask and bottle?
Who mourns for Set or lusting Belphegor?

Who sacrifices meat in Chac-Mool's bowl,
Or bows to humble Hestia in her home?
Who worships Baal with fervent heart and soul?
Do not the sons of Isis rot, unknown?

Astarte waits in vain for mortal prayers
While eight-armed Kali counts her grinning skulls.
Dread Thoth is but a carving on the stairs;
The brass bull Mithras tarnishes and dulls.

Beneath the earth, in fetid catacombs
Lie empty altars, flecked in gold and mud;
My friend, I tell you, once, within those rooms,
Lived mighty gods paid out in lives and blood —

Blood that ran in temples, pooling, seeping,
Gouting from the knives of stone-eyed priests,
Blood of sons and daughters, slack-jawed, weeping,
Slaughtered where they stood, like craven beasts.

And now the lamb of Bethlehem has brought us
The meaning of His Word — yet iron rods
Still bind the mind. All history has taught us
To curse the names of thirty-thousand gods.

Immortals they were called, yet puny man
Still strides the world, their dust beneath his feet.
Let scholars sniff them out as best they can.
I spit upon their graves. Revenge is sweet.

[MUSTIQUE]

'They trouble sleep...'

They trouble sleep, the shadows of the past;
    Thus Magna Carta gnaws at tyrant schemes
While shadows of the present, slantly cast,
    Are what we call the future — in our dreams.

[DORSINGTON]

Xanadu!

I'm certain she were'ent from Porlock,
No more'n from Azerbaijan;
If only I'd fastened me door lock —
(It's murder to rhyme Kubla Khan).

There's times when a man needs amusin',
Lord knows I ain't made outta wood;
But rhymin' while lovin's confusin'—
And niever comes out like it should.

She stormed from me flat like a vandal,
But, Sam, I'm immune to 'er tears,
I think it's a bloody great scandal
Leavin' it two-'undred years.

Jinxed as a Jonah or jammy,
There's nuffin' a man canna' do;
I'm drunk on the milk of it, Sammy!
I'm finishin' off Xanadu!

[MUSTIQUE]

The story of Samuel Taylor Coleridge and the writing of 'Kubla Khan' has been told many times. In 1797, having retired to a lonely farmhouse on Exmoor, Coleridge awoke from a laudanum induced sleep. Seizing pen, ink and paper, he began feverishly scrawling the famous words: 'In Xanadu did Kubla Khan...' Regrettably, he was 'called out' before completing fifty lines 'by a person on business from Porlock'. When he returned to his room an hour later he discovered, to his utter mortification, that while he retained some vague recollection of his vision, he could only complete a further eight or ten lines, petering out on: 'For he on honey-dew hath fed, / And drunk the milk of Paradise.' Thus has 'the person from Porlock' entered the canon of English literature in odium.

Galileo's Dream

There came a voice in dreams, a mighty roar;
My soul grew wings and fled, in terror hurled
Across the airy margins of the world.
Thou See'st Now What None Ere Saw Before!

I clothed my dream in copper and in brass
By candlelight and many a weary day.
One star-filled night, I brushed my fears away
And trembling, placed my eye against the glass.

My first thought was: Alas, 'twas all for nought!
Mere darkness visible, then by degrees
The heavens opened! Dropping to my knees
I cried aloud: *Behold What God Hath Wrought!*

[MUSTIQUE]

[147]

Breakfast on Mustique

Ghost koi, their sunflower-yellow button eyes
Unstitched, weave shadows in the morning sun
And suck on moss-backed stones. The tree ants run
In patrols, their only thought to tyrannise
Some hapless aphid. Scab-red dragon-flies
Patrol just out of reach, jaws set to stun
Their careless prey and drain them, one by one.
Night lilies fold away amidst the cries
Of Bequia-sweets at table, sword-sharp beaks
Extended — each scrap of food defended
From its neighbour. A tortoise heaves and wins
First prize: hibiscus flowers! Our kitten sneaks
Some bacon. The hungry night has ended;
Another day in Paradise begins.

[MUSTIQUE]

Ghost koi are are a pure silver-white variety of ornamental fish. The Japanese call them
Hikarimono or Ogon. Bequia -sweets (*Quiscalus lugubris*) are a form of Carib Grackle, common
throughout the Lesser Antilles. Sharp-eyed, bold and abusive, they squabble interminably.
Bequia, an island close by Mustique, is pronounced 'beckway'.

The Cremation of Jesus Christ

Caelan Fields, Llantrisant, Wales
January 13, 1884

Now stands the Old One, proud, on Caelan Field,
His Druid robe a symbol of his will,
The reek of burning flesh a righteous shield
As grim-faced farmers labour up the hill.

His outstretched arms a silhouette of fire,
He chants in Celtic tongue: "Thus sacrificed,
I now commend unto this funeral pyre
The body of my son, called Jesus Christ!"

His voice rings out in agony and pain;
A burly smith sneers up at him and spits.
The black smoke roils across the sodden plain.
A farmers jeers: "The devil's lost his wits!"

Alone, beside the flames, bereft of hope,
He hurls an errant brand in fiery arc.
Enraged, the screaming mob storms up the slope,
Their brutish faces shining in the dark.

"The land is for the living, not the dead!"
The Druid mocks, "You have no business here!"
"Foul blasphemy!" The single cry is fed
By half a hundred throats as they draw near.

"Not so, you misbegotten Chapel wights —
For those who bury men defile the land!
I choose the fires of old, the ancient rites.
Begone! Or would you kill me where I stand?

"And was it I who saved your wretched lives
When pestilence had laid the village low?
And was it I who visited your wives
In childbirth? Well, was it I, or no?"

A rotten log explodes upon the mound
In showering sparks. The furnace roars anew.
The ragged mob has reached the level ground:
Their leaders halt. The Old One points: "And you!

"Did not I save your daughter when the crones
Abandoned hope — and she now in her prime?
And you! Your broken leg and jagged bones,
I healed them; if you limp, still you can climb!

"Yet I am sore distressed and filled with woe,
My infant son, whom I named Iseu Grist,
Has given up the Ghost. I watched him go.
Fine thanks to bare your teeth and shake your fist!

"Your Chapel *ministers* have urged you here;
Their only mandate — their *authority*!
I see they lead by *skulking* in the rear —
But what am I to them, or they to me?"

A man steps forth, his soot-streaked eyes ablaze,
A hammer in his hairy paw: "Thou liar!
I care not what some heathen Druid says —
'Tis blasphemy! Consign him to the fire!"

Rough hands reach out in earnest as a shrill
Cacophony of whistles pierce the air.
"Police! Police!" the leaping shadows fill
With uniforms —
　I'll end my story there!

※ ※ ※

What's that? You're like to lynch me 'less I tell
At least the Old One's fate? Let this suffice —
Cremation was made legal. All was well.
I wrote these lines to honour
　　　Dr. Price.

[MUSTIQUE]

This is a true story. With embellishments! A plaque on the wall of Zoar Chapel in Llantrisant Reads: 'This tablet was erected by the Federation of British Cremation Authorities, to commemorate the act of Dr. William Price, who cremated the body of his infant son on Caelan Fields. For this act he was indicted on 12th February, 1884, where he was acquitted by Mr. Justice Stephens, who adjudged that cremation was a legal act. Thus was legal sanction given to the practise of cremation.' An eccentric, brilliant and kindly doctor (one of the first to practise homeopathy and scrupulous cleanliness), an ex-Chartist who twice fled the authorities to France where he was forced to live in exile for many years and a believer in nudism, reincarnation, free-love and Druidism, Dr. Price was 83 when he narrowly avoided death on that fateful night. And, yes, his son was called Iseu Grist, Welsh for Jesus Christ. Sadly, Dr. Price does not merit even a note in major encyclopaedias today. His memory deserves better, although he must have many descendants if he was still siring children in his 80's!

'Neither A Lender...'

I do not lend them money now,
(Or very rarely, anyhow).
It saves a friend. And saves a row.

You'd be surprised where friendship ranks
With those who think their friends are banks.
There's far more bricks than roses, thanks!

By some contorted somersault
It all becomes 'your bloody fault'.
It took me years to call a halt.

Some think you mean, some think you shrewd,
Far better that they think you rude
Than suffer their ingratitude.

And wise the man who will not lend,
But in the dead of night will send
A gift. And thus, will save a friend.

[MUSTIQUE]

[153]

'I have a secret servant...'

I have a secret servant
  (My rivals knew I must!)
A loyal thing, and fervent,
  A daemon I can trust.

He sits upon my shoulder,
  Has sat there many a year,
With age, he grows much bolder,
  And whispers in my ear.

And oftentime he's jolly,
  Though if at all ignored
He urges me to folly
  To keep from growing bored.

And sometimes he's indignant,
  Pretending then to weep,
And twice he's grown malignant;
  More often, he's asleep.

But when he senses danger,
  Or fancies easy meat,
God help the hapless stranger
  Who feigns to trick or treat!

He'll take a prince's ransom,
  And dice it — lose or win!
He's small and dark and handsome;
  (He bid me put that in!)

His motto: 'Faster, faster!
   No! Take the other door!'
But which of us is master,
   I've never quite been sure.

Yet I'd not be without him,
   (Though daemons know no friend);
He tells me, (I don't doubt him),
   He'll be there — til the end.

[MUSTIQUE]

Sally Alice

Both rich and poor alike bless Sally Alice.
Oft sickly, still she winks her eye at death.
Her sainted feet tread tenement and palace,
Yet sadder woman never drew a breath.

So answer this: does virtue cleanse its chalice
Of common mirth — like cuckoos in a nest;
Or is it that our laughter, like our malice,
Is rage disguised — mere baggage to the blessed?

[CANDLEWOOD]

Two Plants

Two summer plants grew side by side,
The one grew strong, the other died.

'Too close,' I heard a gardener sigh,
'The yew hedge roots have sucked her dry.

Too late for new to take her place,
The first must shield the empty space.'

Two plants grew in a summer bed,
Then winter came — now both are dead.

[MUSTIQUE]

'The estuaries of hell...'

The estuaries of hell are wide;
　The barges (Satan's special pride)
Provide for those who wish to ride
　One way; for just as advertised
The ferries are all subsidised.

[MUSTIQUE]

Blues

I found my South Side Mecca
By way of Ruislip Mews,
On Parlophone and Decca
Where white boys played the blues.

I spent my spare time lurking
Back stage to pay my dues,
I got my mojo working
With studs who played the blues.

I blew my education,
It wasn't hard to choose,
I passed my graduation
B-minus in the blues.

So if you hear me howlin'
Be sure to spread the news,
I'm howling for my darlin' —
I choose to sing the blues.

[MUSTIQUE]

The first and third lines of the last stanza are lifted almost verbatim from *Howlin' Wolf* (Chester Arthur Burnett) who, for me, represented the epitome of pre-war Mississippi-meets-Chicago blues. *Howlin' Wolf*, his 1962 Chess LP, (known as 'the rocking chair album' because of its cover art), helped to change the course of my life. It was difficult to imagine completing grammar school, going on to college and 'getting a job' after listening to tracks like 'Wang Dang Doodle' and 'Goin' Down Slow'. By my late teens, as a result of constant practice and heavy consumption of untipped French cigarettes, I found myself capable of a passable imitation of Wolf's voice. What audiences made of a half-demented, incomprehensible spotty git belting out 'Smokestack Lightning' and 'Evil Is Going On' in local pubs and clubs is quite another matter. One landlord told me frankly that, in his opinion, I came close to certifiable madness on stage. Looking back, I agree with him. I got laid a lot, though! Howlin' Wolf died in 1976.

'Within a maze...'

Within a maze,
    the path seems never-ending,
How many ways
    there are to lose one's way!
Yet from the air,
    in stately arcs descending,
Dark angels glare,
    impatient at delay.

By day and night
    we shamble, lost in beauty;
Turn left? Turn right?
    Or turn upon a priest?
The Minotaur
    performs his sullen duty;
Beyond the door
    The vultures hop — and feast.

[MUSTIQUE]

Grand-ma

Today he calls me 'grand-ma',
   My hair as white as snow,
But that's not what he called me
   Near fifty year ago;
My curls a fiery tangle,
   My skin a slick of sweat,
My lover riding bare-back
   And we just only met!

When next you're with your grand-ma,
   Try closing half an eye,
Smooth out the wrinkled creases,
   Add lipstick on the sly,
Imagine fiery tresses,
   Imagine there's no dress!
Then save your pity, dearie —
   Been there — done that. Oh yes!

[MUSTIQUE]

A Confrontation in Dorsington
Churchyard, January 1924

You speak to me of patience — take your pick,
Here lie the bones of sundry patient men.
A sweaty hour or so should do the trick;
Your sermons roused 'em once — why not again?

'Death comes to all?' Yes, truly, and the fear
Of righteous hellfire kept 'em all in line.
And now my dear old ma is buried here —
Today, you see the last of me and mine.

The tyranny of church and squire is past!
Three hundred year my folk and all their kin
Have laboured 'by thy leave'. But now, at last
MacDonald and the Labourites are in!

My children read and write as good as you;
They'll not be clearin' up your bloody mess.
Nor fightin' for their king and country, too;
I've left the burial fee — Oh, aye, God Bless!

[MUSTIQUE]

The Door

I hammered hard upon the door, confused,
      My soul in pain:
"What! Am I to be thus abused,
      A pilgrim in the rain?

A dragon-fly with wings still yet to dry
      From Mammon's mire,
May yet outshine a butterfly
      And set the lake a-fire."

But as I raved and battered at the keep
      A voice within
Spoke sweetly to my troubled sleep:
      "'Twas never locked —
        Come in."

[DORSINGTON]

The Bearded Dwarf

There's them as plan and them as chance
And them as rather walk than dance,
There's them as never leaves the shore,
But me, I've always seized an oar,
A mate or two on either side
To set our backs against the tide,
Not knowing where our prow might touch,
Nor turning round, nor caring much.

Strange it is for them as row,
Never seeing where they go,
While lubbers Nelson couldn't teach
Shout out instructions from the beach —
Dry-sailors with their spread-sheet screens
Who count the cost of pork and beans,
New chandlers with their silly lists
Saluting flags and analysts.

I've sailed the ship, I've owned the line,
I've swilled on bilge and drunk fine wine,
I've paced the bloody jetty, too,
Not knowing how I'd pay the crew.
I've sailed at dawn without a plan,
Faced mutiny and 'ung a man,
('ung more than one, if truth be told);
I've stacked the decks with blood and gold
Paid out upon the barrel-head
(With widows *and* their orphans fed
Most scrupulous, 'cash money down' —
I'm quite the thing in Portsmouth Town).

There's men whose backs I 'ad to flay
Who'll tell you I worked 'ard as they,
Stood my watch and stood with ease
While younger men went on their knees;
And though the seas we sail aren't salt,
And though I'm not without some fault,
They line along Canary wharf
To sail upon the *Bearded Dwarf.*

And why? Is it to learn a trade
Or all the filthy gelt we've made?
To 'elp convert our 'eathen kin
Or bang out weevils in a tin?
No sir! It's just they love to mock
The Royal Navy, lock and stock,
To never 'ave to kneel and cow —
Or curtsey on the starboard bow.

There's not a Navy ship that sails
Could 'ope to catch the *Dwarf's* coat tails,
(Unless, the crew was drunk, the sods —
And then I'd give 'em even odds
'Gainst toady jacks who buff the brass
Or kiss the first lieutenant's arse).

No sir! I'd rather starve afloat
Than scoff swill in a Navy boat,
A measly pint of grog a day
And 'Christmas pud on Christmas Day'
If you've behaved — then forced to sing
Like choirboys: 'God Save The King!'

'So up my lads, we're glory bound,
The tide is turning on the Sound,
There's native girls with luscious lips
And nowt but grass upon their hips,
There's Spanish Dons, the old buffoons,
Their fat tubs stuffed with gold doubloons.
Strange stars there are in Southern skies —
Am I a man who'd tell you lies...?

* * *

Line up along Canary wharf:
Sign up to sail the *Bearded Dwarf!*'

[NEW YORK]

Dedicated with heartfelt thanks to all those shipmates who have toiled aboard the *Bearded Dwarf* these past 30 years. She's a fine barky, made finer still by the exceptional talent of the men and women who have crewed her, past and present. I never was much of a captain, I know that. But at least I had the sense to place her in seamanlike hands and retreat to the owner's cabin. (Well, for most of the time, anyway!)

To cOpy-Editers

Pedants resistant to capital letters
Often will soften a point or erase
Barbaric italics to score off their betters —
Lucky for them i was born lower case!

[SOHO]

Whistling Ghosts

Bondsmen grizzled while they chiselled
  Cleopatra's Needle;
Cockneys warbled while they corbelled
  Old St. Paul's Cathedral —

Palaces with Grade I ranking
Once were scaffolding and planking;

Long before the hush of mourners
Workmen spat and shat in corners;

Monuments now called sublime
Were built with blooded sweat and grime;

In rooms which house our royalty
Whistling ghosts still boil their tea.

[SOHO]

Winds That Douse the Candle

If 'out of sight and out of mind' be true
How then may 'absence make the heart leap higher'?
Degrees of feeling reconcile the two:
The winds that douse the candle fan the fire.

[DORSINGTON]

'Hail to the gods of America...'

Hail to the gods of America!
Hail to the gods of the Dream,
Invictus! '*E Pluribus Unum*'!
But which of them reigns supreme?

Which is America's Jupiter?
The brahmins of Capitol Hill?
A sorcerous prophet on Wall Street?
The eye of a Dollar bill?

Or is it it Celebrity Status —
The worship of those we hate,
Or the cult of Living Forever
If only we'd watch our weight?

What of the titans of Media,
Or Hollywood's siren call;
What of the temples of Justice
Whose servants enslave us all?

What of the Brand and the Label?
What of the upstart Sport?
And what of the Constitution,
That bully of last resort?

Hail to the God of America
Whose power the masses extol —
Convenience rules America;
Convenience owns our soul.

[SOHO]

America has done more for me financially than Britain ever has, or ever could have done. Even when on its worst behaviour, I find myself automatically defending the USA from the sneers of green-eyed Europhiles playing their Greek trumps to Roman aces. America is an empire. All empires, by definition, are bumbling, shambolic, bullying, bureaucratic affairs — as certain of the rightness of their cause in infancy as they are corrupted by power in their dotage. I am no historian, but it seems to me that the sins of the USA, compared to those of most previous empires, are of a more moderate — if more pervasive — kind. To put it bluntly, if Americans are so fat, stupid and ignorant, how come they rule the world?

Bedtime Story

'I'll come to thee by moonlight, though hell should
bar the way!' — Alfred Noyes 'The Highwayman'

I was reading him 'The Highwayman'
As he lay tucked up in his bed,
My fingers drumming the horses hooves
On the back of the book as I read;
I read by a ribbon of moonlight
As he turned to me to say:
'I hope that he dodges the soldiers!
Though hell should bar his way!'
But I lost myself in that wild ride
Of a man in a velvet coat —
And when I looked he was fast asleep
With a bunch of sheet at his throat.

[SOHO]

'Love is not compassion...'

Love is not compassion, or a kindness,
 Nor is love attraction steeped in lust;
Friendship and affection lack its blindness:
 Such do as they can — love as it must.

[SOHO]

A World That Was Not There

I turned to find a world that was not there,
Its pages blank, the quisling air grown dumb;
No sign, no sign, all vanished in thin air.

I ransacked drawers and cupboards, all quite bare,
Each finger now had grown into a thumb;
I turned to find a world that was not there.

I stopped to catch my breath and say a prayer
But lost the thread before 'Thy Kingdom come';
No sign, no sign, all vanished in thin air.

I glanced into a mirror in despair,
My lips were mouthing out 'fee fi fo fum';
I turned to find a world that was not there.

I panicked, fled the room and down the stair,
Outside, no trumpets blared, no cymbaled drum;
No sign, no sign, all vanished in thin air.

I joined the throng of those who'd ceased to care,
Our memories now fading, hearts grown numb.
I turned to find a world that was not there;
No sign, no sign, all vanished in thin air.

[SOHO]

'Say this to thyself...'
[for W.E. Henley]

Say this to thyself (beneath thy breath,
    But say it and have be done):
"A mortal's thoughts of dying and death
    Are shadows across the sun."

Say this to thyself (come take some wine,
    'Twas ever the coward's mark):
"There will come the time when I and mine
    Must ferry into the dark."

Say this to thyself (or sing out loud,
    And shatter the windy sky):
"Though sore afraid I shall not be cowed,
    I *live* till the day I *die*."

Say this to thyself (but bail, my friend!
    No boat stayed ever afloat):
"From this day forth to the bitter end
    I shall seize life by the throat."

[DORSINGTON]

'No one ever sang more courageously of life than William Ernest Henley' wrote Louis Untermeyer. He lived much of his life in constant pain, crippled for the last forty years. But even after the death of his daughter he refused to succumb to self-pity and worked on, 'busy and belligerent'. Derided by serious critics of poetry for the sentiment (and, more unforgivably, the popularity) of his most famous poem 'Invictus', Henley spent most of his life as an editor. He made 'many gratifying discoveries among the younger writers.' His later poetry, especially the moving 'Margaritae Sorori', suggests that he might have done better to explore his own talents as a poet more fully.

Johnson

[for Robert L. Johnson]

I sat last night in Soho
    Blues falling down like hail,
The Devil in falsetto,
    A hellhound on his trail.

The words came helter-skelter,
    Long fingers fiddling fire,
Your soul is in the Delta,
    When Johnson bends the wire.

They say he bought tuition
    From Satan on the sly,
But that's just superstition;
    Still, when he came to die,

When Hell's lieutenant coshed him
    To take him fair and square,
I bet young Johnson joshed him:
    'You got guitars down there?'

[SOHO]

The first time I heard Robert Johnson *(King of the Delta Blues)* in 1966 on vinyl, the hair stood up on the back of my head. It still does. Here is talent and musical virtuosity made flesh, salted with hints of madness and voodoo intimations of mortality. He died in his middle twenties, his whisky poisoned, so they say, by a jealous rival. I once came across a quote concerning the worth of an artist's life (Keats in this case) measured against the lives of their contemporaries: "Ode on a Grecian Urn is worth any number of old ladies." Political correctness proscribes such elitist sentiment today, but Robert Johnson's genius could lead me into the shadow of temptation damn easily!

Old Dog, New Trick

I am an old dog which has learned a new trick
Concerning the secrets of sunlight. This trick
Will not improve one's pension
Or aid in the prevention
Of indignities to come when one grows sick —
Sick of a world grown sick of an old dog sick
Of being sick. But still, it is a *new* trick.

You must sit by quiet water, in the sun,
In the morning or the evening. Said sun
Must fall in such direction
As angles its reflection
From the water to your eye. This being done,
Squeeze both eyelids tightly shut. *This* being done,
Be still. There will come an image of the sun —

But in such colours! And there's a further trick:
Take a battered hat to wear. This added trick
Keeps diamond light from fading
While colours come cascading,
In cataracts. In a while you may feel sick —
Sick of a world grown sick of an old dog sick
Of being sick.   But still, it is a *new* trick.

[DORSINGTON]

Fundamentals

The fruits of the Crusaders haunt us still,
'Creationism' slithers from its hole,
They'd kill us all to save one mortal soul
While heathen unbelievers foot the bill.
Priest, wherein lies the freedom in 'free-will',
The gift of which was never yours to dole?
You but return to men what first you stole
With hints of paradise to coat the pill.
Your certainties speak love but end in death:
The mullahs bay for blood in Babylon,
In Bethlehem the Hebrews marshal tanks.
A pox on every martyr who drew breath —
Hard sermons do but urge the rabble on
While men in balaclavas smirk their thanks.

[NEW YORK]

[172]

Charlotte

*[Time Future whispers in
Charlotte Mew's ear]*

There's ash a-plenty in London town,
Oh, Charlotte — stay your hand!
Retie those ribbons, put them down —
Your 'second-best' be damned.

A blemished pot, the clay misthrown?
Well, what are editors *for*?
Perfection lies with God alone —
Just toss them in a drawer.

A feminine rhyme grown scandalous,
It's veil beyond repair?
These midnight hours are perilous
For poets in despair.

Have done with pride, this urge to burn,
To tamper and to shred —
In fifty years the tide will turn;
Oh, Charlotte — go to bed!

[MUSTIQUE]

Less than sixty poems by Charlotte Mew survive — and yet we know she wrote many, many more. Her life was plagued with unhappiness compounded by repressed sexuality and a fear of hereditary insanity. Despite encouragement from one or two prominent poets, (Hardy called her 'the best woman poet of our time'), her talent was generally unappreciated until after her suicide in 1928. Worse still, Charlotte Mew's striving for perfection and, perhaps, her wish to conceal any trace of lesbian eroticism, led her to destroy nearly all her 'second-best' work. Friends later claimed she had 'trunks full of them'. She was even reported as using these old manuscripts to light cigarettes from the fire. For anyone who has ever read 'The Farmer's Wife' or 'I Have Been Through The Gates', this represents a profound loss to English poetry. If you have not yet discovered Charlotte Mew, I envy you!

[173]

The Lamb Bids the Tyger Farewell

The poet has come to the pamphleteer
  Most secretly, most secretly,
The Lamb has spoke in the Tyger's ear:
  'I fear for thee. I fear for thee.

'The noose is looped on the Liberty Tree!
  A tyrant's rope, a tyrant's rope,
The Lion has loosed the Jackals. Flee!
  Thy only hope, thy only hope.'

The Tyger has taken the poet's arm
  His face is wry, his face is wry:
'And wilt thou come, O lamb of alarm?'
  'No, no, not I. No, no, not I.

'Oh, but I shall pen such a verse this day,
  To make amend, to make amend,
As shall shake the world in another way —
  Farewell, my friend; farewell, my friend.'

[NEW YORK]

In 1792, William Blake came to warn the fiercely radical activist and writer, Thomas Paine, that the British authorities were about to arrest him for treason following publication in London of the second part of Paine's *The Rights of Man*. Paine fled to Dover and took ship to France with the arrest party literally on his heels. Had they caught him, he would certainly have been hung — as his subsequent trial *in abstentia* made clear. Paine went on to take a significant role in the French revolution, just as he had in the American colonies, where his pamphlet, *Common Sense*, was influential in bringing about the Declaration of Independence. William Blake published *The Tyger* (Tyger, Tyger, burning bright / In the forests of the night...) in 1794 in *Songs of Experience*. Of course, the conceit that The Tyger in any way portrays Thomas Paine is merely that — as every scholar of Blake would affirm. Yet reading the poem again with the thought in mind made me wonder...

Of Walls and Fences

Of wrong or right I scorn to sing
(Philosophy pays less than pence),
I sing me of a little thing
Contemptible to common sense —
The rightness of a wall or fence.

If privacy is precious stuff
Then walls exclude a neighbour, true;
Except it puts them in a huff,
And, even worse, it spoils the view.
Such fences need maintaining, too.

Why envy what we cannot see?
But cant comes easy to the pen —
Men's lives are warped by property,
I've strung barbed wire, and will again.
A wall brings out the worst in men.

[MUSTIQUE]

[177]

Love Came to Visit Me

Love came to visit me,
  Shy as a fawn,
But finding me busy,
  She fled with the dawn.

At twenty, the torch of
Resentment was lit,
My rage at injustice
Waxed hot as the pit,
The flux of its lava
Cleared all in its path,
Comrades and enemies
Fled from its wrath.
Yet lovers grew wary
Once novelty waned —
To lie with a panther
Is terror unfeigned.

At thirty, my powers
Seemed mighty to me,
The fruits of my rivals
I shook from the tree,
By guile and by bluster
By night and by day
I battered and scattered
The fools from my way;
And women grew willing
To sham and to bluff —
Their trinkets and baubles
Cost little enough.

From forty to fifty,
Grown easy and sly
I wined 'em and dined 'em;
Like pigs in a sty
We feasted and revelled
And rutted in muck,
Forgetting our peril,
Forgetting to duck,
Forgetting time's arrows
Are sharper than knives,
Grown sick to our stomachs —
And sick of our lives.

Love came to visit me,
Shy as a fawn,
But finding me busy,
She fled with the dawn.

[MUSTIQUE]

Fin Finis

[A Shanty for a Harpooned Whale]

Haul away,
> *Haul away,*
>> *My proud bully boys, haul away.*

A whale knows
> That you know
>> As he knows
What only the prophets foresaw;
>> When at Gaia's last turn,
>> At entropy's burn —
Whales will walk as they once walked before.

Haul away,
> *Haul away,*
>> *My proud bully boys, haul away.*

A whale dreams
> That you dream
>> Of her dreams;
Of spume and of krill and of claw;
>> Of cold Arctic moons,
>> Of exploding harpoons —
And of fires that will crack the sea floor.

Haul away,
> *Haul away,*
>> *My proud bully boys, haul away.*

Oh, two legs,
     Or four legs
          Or no legs,
The helix runs false at its core;
     As the sun slowly dies,
     As the boiling seas rise —
Whales will dance on the ocean's last shore.

Haul away,
     Haul away,
          My proud bully boys, haul away.

[DORSINGTON]

'A miser's purse...'

A miser's purse may nurse
     A poet's pen;
I've supped with pigs whose verse
     Would break your heart —
     And slept with wall-eyed sluts
          Who spoke of Zen:
Men's lives are not their own,
     Still less their art.

[CANDLEWOOD]

'You may not evil do...'

You may not evil do, that good be hurled
    To heal a greater wound. Upon such hope
Has balanced half the malice of the world,
    And toppled, headlong, down its fatal slope.

[MUSTIQUE]

In 1956, the philosopher, Elizabeth Anscombe (1919 -2001) objected to the conferment of an honorary degree upon ex-President Harry Truman (because of his decision to drop the atomic bomb on Hiroshima) with the words: 'You may not do evil that good may come.' The original expression, as far as I can trace it, came from *Some Fruits of Solitude* by William Penn (1644-1718), Quaker founder of Pennsylvania: 'To do evil that good may come of it is for bunglers in politics as well as morals.'

She Got What She Wanted

*(But She Lost What She Had)**

Worried sick that I might never
know what I know
now,
Fed up with my best friend's bragging,
(bloody-minded
cow);

I took ignorance and shook it,
rattling its
teeth;
Made a two-backed beast and took a
tumble (with a
sheath!);

Innocence slid like a nylon
nightie to the
floor;
'Nice tits!' leered carnal knowledge
oiling out the
door.

[MUSTIQUE]

*Title from a song recorded by the inimitable
Little Richard in the late 50's*

Seek-no-further
[The Walking Apple Tree]

Down the hillsides of New England
Apple blossoms scent the air;
Seek-no-further farmers call 'em;
English settlers put 'em there.

Planted 'em high up the mountains,
Knowing 'em a tasty bite,
Knowing when an old tree rotted
It must fall one wintry night;

Knowing that its shoots and branches
Walk the hills and spring anew;
Seek-no-further farmers call 'em:
If you ate 'em, you would, too!

[DORSINGTON]

I first came across the story of *Seek-no-further* apple trees in Eric Sloane's book A *Reverence for Wood* published in 1965. According to Mr. Sloane, the first such tree was planted 'in the 1700's in Westfield, Massachusetts on top of Dudleytown Mountain' by an English settler who had brought the seeds from Cornwall. Over the centuries these trees, which have the habit of re-rooting their branches when they collapse from old age, have gradually crept down the slopes in various parts of New England, especially Pennsylvania. They are still to be found, sometimes known as Westfields. Until the early part of last century, farmers would occasionally take their family up into the mountains to graft Westfields onto wild crabs. If Mr. Sloane's folk-lore is true, there may well be apple trees in New England which, in a sense, are three hundred years old. It is a fancy of mine to bring back a handful of wild *Seek-no-further* seeds or layerings across the Atlantic and plant them here in England — on a hillside, of course!

Atlas Shrugs

As mass extinctions come and go,
    They sneer at Michelangelo;
Shakespeare's genius is just
    A rumour to volcanic dust.

Bacilli and fungal spores
    Lose no sleep on Newton's Laws;
Nor do polar ice-caps learn
    Of odes upon a Grecian Urn.

Neither moon nor asteroid
    Alters course for Jung or Freud;
Atlas shrugs and rolls his eyes
    When hairless apes philosophise.

[MUSTIQUE]

Swim or Float

Wise men advise we float the stream of life:
    "All folly lies in wishes unfulfilled."
It's clear that wise men never had a wife,
    Or ever poured a glass of Chablis — chilled!

[SOHO]

Dream Time

Within a dream I watched a city rise
  To thrive a thousand years in craft and power,
And mourned to see its wreck through god-like eyes:
  Yet woke to find I'd slept but half an hour.

Time tramples on, the years roll by in ranks
  No less upon the wicked than the blessed,
How is it then that dreams, like armoured tanks,
  Reverse the trick, their centuries compressed?

[CANDLEWOOD]

God Knows What

  Much easier by far to shrug of course,
  When some fool asks: Do you believe in God?
  No river ever ran without a source —
  I've always found the question rather odd.

  Theology was writ by mortal men;
  Their faith and funny hats are all they've got.
  When all is said and done they rule by pen;
  For certain something's there
          — but God knows what.

[MUSTIQUE]

'Though no good deed...'

Though no good deed escapes due punishment,
Yet kindness in a naughty world endures;
The ripples of its pebbled sediment
Betray the shoals that wickedness obscures.

[DORSINGTON]

Deducing Fairies

The tide of contradiction swirls and foams
    Unceasingly, lest mortal thought should harden;
What demons drove the don of Sherlock Holmes
    To fairies at the bottom of the garden?

[MUSTIQUE]

The simplistic answer to that question is the death of Sir Arthur Conan Doyle's son from wounds incurred in the First World War. Doyle's interest in spiritualism blossomed into an obsession which led him to support several charlatans, despite a public pose of scrupulous 'authentication' towards spiritualist claims. The 'fairies at the bottom of the garden' was one such case. Pictures of 'the little people' were cut out and photographed in a garden setting by mischievous children. For years their authenticity was a subject of serious debate. What the abrupt, analytical Holmes would have made of such nonsense is best left to the imagination. For me, however, Doyle is still the greatest writer of detective fiction who ever lived — and be damned to the fairies!

Neanderthal Nights

And if out walking on a summer's night
Up Coxcombe Hill, the stars for company,
A bellyfull of beer to comfort me,
I should chance to see in the bleached moonlight
One of the Old Ones, hairy, arms locked tight
Around some piggy-backed monstrosity
Perched upon her shoulder, loping casually
Across the Downs as if the ancient flight
Of all her kind was but an old wives' tale —
What then? Might I lie hid beside the trail,
My ferulled walking stick a flint-tipped spear?
Or should I step in view, supressing fear,
Professing brotherhood? (Not in this song:
I've read the Old One's memories were long!)

[MUSTIQUE]

Seven-legged Spider

Beside my desk there rests the noble NOD
Upon whose blue and silver spine this morn
I watched unfold a mystery of God,
A seven-legged spider squirming to be born —
Or should I say re-born — his useless husk
Discarded on the 'g' while he ran straight
Around the board into the shadowed dusk.
I counted out his legs, and there were eight
(Though one was but a nub — 'twill doubtless grow
When he at last emerges from his lair).
Is sacrifice, then, all we need to know
Of life's perfection? Gods of fire and air!
  I'd cast my midwife NOD into the brine
  To thus repair this crippled verse of mine.

[CANDLEWOOD]

The New Oxford Dictionary of English, (the **NOD**), is, to my mind, the best new single volume
dictionary of British English in print. For years, I had thought those husks of spiders occasionally
found in empty wastepaper bins were their desiccated bodies. Not so, apparently!   Like crabs,
some leave their dried out carapace behind in order to grow larger — or to replace a missing limb.

Telex Memories

The click of the keys as we hit 'em,
The smell as the paper unrolled,
The messages squeezed so we'd fit 'em,
The whine of the clutch as it scrolled;

The clatter of traffic incoming,
The heading 'Most Urgent - Reply',
The rattling, beeping and humming:
'Two minutes. Encoding. Stand By!'

[DORSINGTON]

Throughout the 1960's, 70's and well into the 80's, a telex (probably a Western Union model) was an indispensable piece of office kit. Long before computers migrated from air conditioned 'clean rooms' controlled by men in white coats to desk tops, the only sensible and secure method for a company to communicate long distances was by telex. Long distance telephone calls were ruinously expensive and air-mail post too slow. One would first reduce the message to the shortest possible length - often using code and jargon - then type it into a telex keyboard and finally push a button or pull a switch to send it to another telex machine, thousands of miles away. As the machines were electromechanical, one got used to their idiosyncrasies — rather like early cars which had to be started or driven in a certain way to ensure they worked at all. The message from a telex was printed out on rolls of paper (sometime coloured yellow) and requests for an immediate reply were common. It sounds almost pathetic now, but this feeling of being in communication with another person half way around the world was really exciting! The fax machine, of course, put telex communication out of business virtually overnight in most Western countries. I loved 'em!

The Old, Old Error

Think you — full certain all men must embark
    And slip their cabled moorings from this place
To journey, Christ knows where, upon the dark —
    That He will make exception, in your case?

[DORSINGTON]

The Snowman

He was sitting by the tow-path on a stump,
   Like a moonlit sihouette,
With the snow settling softly on his shoulders.
   'Bout eleven more mile, yet!'
He hailed, pointing with his pipe down river.
   Swinging the prow midstream
I spun the wheel to broach the white-flaked wind
   And brought her hard a-beam,
Kissed the jetty, cut the engines, grabbed a rope
   And reached to tie the cord
Around a ringbolt. 'I'll take that, you lubber,'
   Wheezed the snowman. 'Back aboard
And sling me down the other from the blunt end.'
   Ten minutes later we
Were sitting in the cabin, sipping tea. Outside
   The snow fell silently
And a frosted moon slipped in and out of clouds
   Fringed by nodding Norfolk reeds.
'I be the local ferryman' — so he told us:
   'Where the Great Black Mere feeds
The Yare, a ferry's stood for nigh five hundred year.'
   He bid us moor the night
If we should want, then gravely took his leave,
   A gaunt, archaic sight
With his oil-lit lantern bobbing through the gloom
   And a tread as soft...as soft...
Suddenly all the hairs on the back of my head
   Stood up and racing aloft

I found us floating free, the ropes limp down the sides,
   The 'jetty' but a spit of mud.
Gunning up the engines I reversed, half thrust,
   The fear fierce in my blood
And called our for a torch. We played it on the banks
   Amid the freezing air
But though we searched and searched and searched again
   There were no footprints there,
Nor ringbolts. In the pub that night at Yarmouth
   We asked a local at the inn
If he'd heard of a ferry by the Great Black Mere:
   'No,' he shrugged, with an evil grin.

[MUSTIQUE]

In Time of Doubt

Outcast stands my Bible on the shelf
Beside the prince of darkness there,
It leans as though to warm itself
Upon the bonfires of Voltaire.
And if I thought that Ferney's wraith
Could thus adjust such lack of faith
I'd pluck the pair and weigh them out:
The both for wit, but which for doubt?

[SOHO]

*Ferney was the estate purchased by Voltaire in 1758
just over the French border from Geneva.*

You!

*[Against all orders, Beelzebub, Lord of Flies and Satan's Chief Lieutenant,
visits the dreams of mortals soon to be his master's guest]*

You! You grinning parasite!
       Lounging on your Hepplewhite,
       Sharpening your cut-glass vowels;
       Hell will revel in your howls
       While demons dine upon your bowels.
                 I warrant you'll grin then a'right...
                 (You've got until tomorrow night!)

You! You windbag sycophant!
       Lord of blather, king of cant,
       Polishing your sly replies;
       Behold the altar of your lies!
       Here busy tongues are thick with flies
                 And used — it rhymes with excellent...
                 (Two days, you piece of excrement!)

You! My little chickadee!
       My master's given you to me!
       Blabber mouthing smut and dirt,
       Wallowing in others' hurt;
       Immersed in worse, your lips will blurt
                 And vomit gossip endlessly...
                 (Three weeks, and then eternity!)

You! Ah yes, the chosen few!
       Certain I cannot be true,
       Struggling to wake and shout:
       Hearken to the maggot doubt,
       Lest when your soul go walkabout
                 You find what wiser prophets knew...
                 (Beelzebub waits here for you!)

[CANDLEWOOD]

[194]

'When the boot goes in...'

When the boot goes in,
When the boot goes in,
When you sink it in in with all o'your force
It's better than sex-u-al intercourse —

When the boot goes in,
When the boot goes in,
When you hear the cartilage snap and pop
And the bastard's begging for you to stop —

When the boot goes in,
When the boot goes in,
When you ken the scumbag hasn't a chance,
And he's rolled in a ball and shat in his pants —

It's better than when the Rangers win!
When the boot goes in,
When the boot goes in.

[MUSTIQUE]

[Please recite in a Glaswegian accent!]

In the mid-seventies my friend and co-author, Don Atyeo, contracted to write a book called *Blood and Guts: Violence in Sport*. He returned from his research trip to Scotland a shaken man. In Glasgow he had managed to hook up with a bunch of psychopaths whose greatest pleasure in life was to attend soccer matches armed to the teeth with metal pipes, knives, hatchets and even — one of them confided — a sword. Don was not unnaturally terrified in the company of these maniacs, knowing himself protected only their sense of flattery that a foreigner was writing a book about them. He was hardly surprised, then, when their drunken leader told him that the best — the very best — feeling in the world was not when he attacked rivals with a weapon in his hand, but the anticipation of sinking his boot in somebody's guts. It was, he confessed, *sotto voce*, 'better than sex-u-al intercourse'.

Lord North Instructs His Son and Heir...

[on the latter's 18th birthday]

And are we loved, my boy? And has the Pope
    Turned Protestant?   Do pigs spring wings to fly?
    Is there a man among us makes reply?
The lower orders dream of noosing rope
Around our barbered necks! They live in *hope,*
    While we live at our *ease.* You wonder why?
    I'll tell you then, the trick, and you may ply
Your adolescence scruples up the slope
    Of men's debate. The answer is that *fear,*
Dear boy — make note! — is stronger meat by far
    Than envy. Thus, the aristocracy
    Has ruled time out of mind. *Fear knows no peer!*
Forget this for an instant and our star
    Must sink into the swamp, DEMOCRACY!

....Who Replies Thirty Years Later

[by his fathers tomb]

And were you loved, my Lord? And was the price
    Sufficient for the ferryman to heed —
    Or sent you sullen surfs upon stampede
To storm the very gates of paradise?
I mean no disrespect. It must suffice
    That any son could conjure such a deed
    At such a time. I fear, my Lord, your seed
Is sadly sunk. The fire has met the ice
    And one suspects the breed is near extinct.
Times change, magnetic NORTH has turtled poles
    As rivers now run uphill to the weir.
    The Whigs have stared us out and we have blinked,
While merchant pigs defile the honour rolls —
    Truth is, my father dear, *this peer knows fear.*

[MUSTIQUE]

Classic Clichés

Why do lies come wrapped in tissues?
Who would push an open door?
Am I really 'Yours sincerely'
When we've never met before?

Why is elegance always classic?
Why is frost a man called Jack?
Who has ever begged your pardon?
See *what* monkey on your back?

Are *all* suspects armed and dangerous?
Where's this level playing-field?
When is the eleventh hour?
Are the fates of all men *sealed?*

Why do people say 'Don't go there'
When you've never left the room?
When were you last bored to tears?
Why must prophets foretell doom?

Ever seen a wood that's treeless?
Why is envy always green?
Why is life a bitch, you bastard?
Can the whole nine yards be seen?

What's it all about then, Alfie?
By and large, I'd have to say,
When the rock has met the hard place —
Leave no stone unturned — OK?

[SOHO]

Flower Power

[For Pearl Bicar]

Came the Friday — came the dragon
    Up the stairs with fire and broom:
'Rent is *late*, young man,' she scolded.
    What's this? *Flowers* in your room!'

On an impulse, feeling guilty,
    I plucked out a splendid bloom:
'Would you take these, Mrs. Harris,
    Take some flowers for your room?'

Half a weary life had flown by
    (Oh, *but she remembered whom!*)
Since a lad had brought her flowers,
    Pretty flowers for her room.

She forgave me, smiling oddly;
    Strange, how dragons cease to fume.
Off she marched to find fresh water
    For the flowers in her room.

✻

Always look beneath the armour,
    Make a rule from womb to tomb:
Take the time to smell the roses,
    Keep some flowers in your room!

[SOHO]

'You think it made a difference...'

You think it made a difference
   To try, like Robert Frost,
To take the road less travelled,
   To play at getting lost?

Or was it more by accident,
   (I know it was for me),
The ox-bow lakes of habit
   Meandering to the sea?

You think they make a difference,
   These choices by default?
No matter to the ocean —
   It turns all water salt.

[MUSTIQUE]

Acknowledgements

PERMISSION FROM Viking Penguin, a division of Penguin Books USA and Gerald Duckworth & Co. Ltd, to reprint *Résumé* by Dorothy Parker is gratefully acknowledged.

As most of my poetry is composed to be recited aloud, I have tested the patience and affection of numerous close friends and colleagues, using them as guinea-pigs. Without their encouragement and gentle mockery I would not have had the courage to publish *A Glass Half Full* — nor, perhaps, the discipline to revise many of the poems over and over again. Let me thank them all here, sincerely and unreservedly.

While on the subject of revisions, excisions, excesses and decisions, let me offer rueful, heartfelt thanks to my editor, Simon Rae. Undaunted by bluster, immovable in the face of blandishments and susceptible only to reasoned argument and the odd glass of Bordeaux, his scholarly and wise counsels have rescued me time and again.

Stan and Elizabeth Clayton, who own Firefly Guest House in Mustique, first persuaded me to read my poetry in public. As I now do so at the drop of a hat, I am not precisely certain how much of a favour they did the world, but it meant the world to me.

Many of my colleagues at Dennis Publishing in London and New York have risked their careers with serious and constructive advice. Ditto for the staff of my private office and residences who kept the world at bay for a precious few weeks when I needed it most.

The team who helped me enter the arcane world of the spoken word are listed within the CD jacket, but I must especially thank Gerry Healy and George Taylor for their patience and technical wizardry. My old friend Richard Adams came through on the design front along with Mike Dunn on page design. As I have no literary agent, Gail Rebuck and Simon Master helped me to find a wonderful publisher, Sue Freestone, at Hutchinson. She has been a tower of strength to a bumbling amateur. Perhaps literary agents should be abolished immediately.

Lastly, I owe a debt to the late Michael Nixon, who urged me — quite literally on his deathbed, as he had for several years before that — to seek for 'What Lies Hidden'. I have tried, my old friend, I have truly tried.